Exploring America's Future

Exploring America's Future

Douglas Caddy

Texas A&M University Press

College Station

Library of Congress Cataloging-in-Publication Data

Caddy, Douglas, 1938–
  Exploring America's future.
  Includes index.
  1. United States—Forecasting. I. Title.
E169.12.C23 1987   303.4'973   86-23072
ISBN 0-89096-271-5

Manufactured in the United States of America
First Edition

Contents

List of Tables / vii

Preface / ix

1 The Economics of Change / 3

2 The Late, Great Society / 35

3 A Religious Awakening? / 67

4 Notes on the American System of Education / 97

5 Politics in the Postindustrial Era / 121

6 The Future of Warfare / 151

Index / 177

Tables

1. Postindustrial Employment Opportunities, / 25–26

2. U.S. Total Fertility Rate and Intrinsic Rate
of Natural Increase, / 47

3. Median Years of School Completed, by Race, / 61

4. Comparative Military Strength,
NATO and Warsaw Pact, / 160

5. Comparative Nuclear Strength,
Warsaw Pact and NATO, / 161

Preface

All attempts to predict the future in any detail
appear ludicrous within a few years.
                                    —Arthur C. Clarke

Almost every student has had at least one educator whose
manner of teaching and the knowledge imparted have left an
indelible imprint in the student's mind. In my case the teacher
was Prof. Carroll Quigley, who taught "Introduction to Civilization" to those of us in the freshman class at Georgetown
University's School of Foreign Service. We never willingly
missed Professor Quigley's lectures; we always left his lecture
hall feeling intellectually richer for the experience.

Fortunately for posterity, Professor Quigley was an outstanding author as well as an able teacher. One of his books, *The
Evolution of Civilizations: An Introduction to Historical
Analysis* (New York: Macmillan, 1961) records the erudition
he showed in his classroom. It is his basic historical framework that I have attempted to follow here. In his work Professor Quigley writes,

> We could, indeed, divide this gamut (of the range of hu-
> man potentialities) into forty or into four hundred divi-
> sions or levels, since the reality with which our worlds
> seek to deal is a subtle, continuous, and flexible range
> quite beyond our ability to grasp clearly or fully. This
> range of human potentialities will be divided in [*The
> Evolution of Civilizations*], for purpose of historical
> analysis, into six levels, as follows: (1) military, (2) politi-
> cal, (3) economic, (4) social, (5) religious and (6) intellec-

ix

tual, although this division will always be made with the full realization that it could with good justification, be made otherwise as five, seven, sixty or six hundred levels. (p. 17)

Exploring America's Future attempts to analyze future trends by using Professor Quigley's historical methodology for analyzing past civilizations. I have used all of his six levels, changing only the last, "intellectual," to "education." I did this because I felt that analyzing trends in education was a safer guide to what the future holds than is present intellectual activity.

For you who thirst for greater knowledge about the future, I suggest you write to the World Future Society, 4916 St. Elmo Avenue, Bethesda, Md. 28014-5089. Its publications and meetings make it a most worthwhile organization.

I wish also to take this occasion to express my personal appreciation to the trustees of the Moody Foundation of Galveston, Texas—Mrs. Mary Moody Northen, Robert Moody, and Shearn Moody, Jr.—whose foundation grant to the Texas A&M University Press made possible the writing of this book.

I also wish to thank for their assistance the following four individuals: Texas A&M University professor Henry C. Dethloff, Michael Smith, Allan C. Brownfeld, and Robert Tanner.

Exploring America's Future

CHAPTER ONE

The Economics of Change

Nothing endures but change. —Heraclitus

The world's economy has entered its "third wave," or the age of "high tech." The modern industrial cycle of the past half century has ended and a "postindustrial" cycle has begun. New industry organized around information and data processing, telecommunications, genetic engineering, services, and space have emerged as the dynamic factors in the new postindustrial economic order. Will there be enough food, nonfuel minerals, water, and energy for survival or possibly for a more broadly based affluence over the next half century? What will be the impact of "deindustrialization" on how we work and live? What the high tech age means for our future, for the next fifty years, is the subject of the 1982 *Global 2000 Report to the President*, and a private study called *The Resourceful Earth*, completed in 1984. Two different futures emerge.

What does the future hold? Is thought about the future merely idle speculation and fantasizing? Or can we, by attempting to understand the major factors that have shaped our past and necessarily affect our future in some way, project what our future might reasonably be? Although it may well be true that nothing endures but change, can we become the agents of constructive change rather than merely the victims of that change?

The modern economist would certainly describe the world economy as in a state of change and flux. The relatively stable economic growth in industrialized and many developing coun-

3

tries during the 1950s and 1960s was severely altered during the economic upheavals of the seventies. The recessions of the 1970s, and most recently that of 1981–1983, caused some people to believe that a new "Great Depression" was just around the corner. There is little comparison, however, between the Great Depression and the economic disturbances of more recent decades. A report issued by the World Bank in 1983, for example, explains that between 1929 and 1932 the aggregate Gross Domestic Product (GDP) of advanced countries fell 17.1 percent and world trade by 26.8 percent. In contrast, in the 1974–1975 recession, GDP declined 0.4 percent and world trade 5.0 percent. In 1981–1982, the GDP of industrial countries rose slightly and world trade fell by only 1 percent.[1]

Although the recessionary periods of the 1970s, fueled by inflation and skyrocketing energy costs, did not approximate in effect the Great Depression of the 1930s, the impact of these negative economic developments was nevertheless significant. At the end of the 1970s many of the industrialized nations discovered that the once-steady base on which their economies were founded, that is, heavy manufacturing, had begun what many analysts were referring to as a "major shift." Alvin Toffler referred to the shift as a "third wave."[2] Others called it the advent of the age of "high-tech."

What brought about this somewhat sudden shift from an industrial economy to a postindustrial or high-tech economy? One can easily surmise, when viewing economic shifts in broad historical patterns, that the current shift is the result of passing from one economic cycle to another. The previous economic cycle began around the mid-1930s and was highlighted by the development and expansion of manufacturing industries relating to oil and petroleum products, automobiles and aviation, and finally television and computers.

The Modern Industrial Cycle

The modern industrial cycle followed the Great Depression and was hastened by the enormous demand for manufactured

1. The World Bank, *World Development Report* (London: Oxford University Press, 1983), p. 20.
2. Alvin Toffler, *The Third Wave* (New York: Morrow & Co., 1984).

goods created by World War II. Soon after the post–World War II recession caused by labor dislocations, industrial reconversion, inflation, and general confusion, the economy began a period of rapid expansion. Enforced wartime savings were poured into consumer purchasing power and into capital for industrial expansion. Regional markets became worldwide markets, in part under the auspices of the Marshall Plan, which poured some seventy-three billion dollars into European economies between 1948 and 1960. Raw materials were available, accessible, and relatively inexpensive. The expansionary phase of the modern industrial economic cycle lasted for approximately twenty years, or until the mid-1960s.

The third phase of this cycle began about 1965 and lasted until 1975. It is best described as a period of matured growth, with the GDP of industrial and developing countries still expanding, but at a reduced rate. During this stage many industries saw their profit margins cut and witnessed increased competition, surplus production capacity, and rising debt. In the final stage, between approximately 1975 and 1985, the economy entered a period of decline characterized by dwindling amounts of investment capital, growing obstacles to free trade, rising unemployment levels, and an alarming number of bankruptcies.

These four stages of the modern industrial economic cycle took nearly fifty years to evolve. Two critical factors hastened the end of the modern industrial economic cycle—the oil shortage and inflation. Whereas oil- and petroleum-related industries fueled the economic expansion of the 1950s and 1960s, the oil shortage of the seventies raised serious doubts about the adequacy of worldwide energy supplies. The oil shortage produced a massive shift in the balance of trade from the United States and its Western-bloc trading partners to the members of the OPEC (Organization of Petroleum Exporting Countries) cartel.

The dramatic trade realignment halted Western expansion and fueled inflation. As the balance of payments shifted amid signs of rapid deterioration in the economies of the United States and some of its trading partners, a "crisis in confidence" began in world financial markets. The value of the dollar began to decline relative to other currencies. With the drop of the dollar and the rapid increase of oil prices, the cost of manufacturing rose, and prices rose in the marketplace. Confidence in world capital markets continued to decline, and large amounts of international funds were withdrawn from the U.S. banking system. To compensate for the shrinking of funds in the banking system of the United States, the Federal Reserve Board (the U.S. equivalent of a central bank) increased the amount of currency in circulation ("MI," as it is called in financial circles). The increase in MI was designed to avoid the choking off of capital supplies and thus to keep the measure of supply/demand within credit markets, that is, interest rates and the value of money, stable. But, as often is the case, the policy of the Federal Reserve had the opposite effect.[3]

By increasing MI (printing more money), the Federal Reserve diluted the real value of the dollar. This meant that the present value of a dollar was worth more than it would be at some future time. Interest rates are a function of supply versus the demand for funds. The supply of funds, that is, the number of individuals and institutions willing to lend a required amount of money, is determined by another function, risk versus return. Because investors felt that the dollars they lent out would be returned at a diluted value due to inflation, they demanded a higher return (interest) for their risk. Therefore, with fewer investors willing to take on the risk of inflation, and with those who did requiring a higher rate of return, interest rates climbed to unprecedented levels in modern economic times.

As we passed into the decade of the 1980s the Federal Reserve began to compensate for its previous mistake of allowing the money supply to grow beyond reasonable limits. Several countries followed the U.S. lead and decided to clamp down on inflation by capping the growth of their money supply. The short-term results were almost catastrophic. Interest rates remained high and unemployment shot up to the highest levels since the Great Depression. Construction levels dropped, plant capacity utilization sank to its lowest levels, and the number of bankruptcies skyrocketed.

All of these factors had international as well as domestic dimensions. For example, the growth rate of GDP in develop-

3. See Maxwell Newton, *The Fed* (New York: New York Times Press, 1984).

ing countries declined from 6.3 percent in 1960–1973 to only 1.95 percent in 1980–1983. Unemployment in seven major industrial countries rose from 2.7 percent in 1965, to 8 percent in 1983. Inflation in the same countries had risen from 2.7 percent in 1965 to a peak of 12.2 percent before beginning a decline in the eighties. Increases in government spending as a share of GDP went from 29.3 percent in 1962 to 40.9 percent in 1981, removing funds for industrial development from capital markets. Finally, there was a dramatic decline in the real rates of return on capital of corporations in a number of the major industrial nations, with many businesses experiencing a decline in profitability.[4]

With all of these negative developments, many economists and other prognosticators began to predict continued stagnation and even world economic collapse. But there is growing evidence that these dire prophecies were premature.

The Post-industrial Cycle

What we seem to have, rather than economic collapse, is the end of an old economic order and the beginning of a new economic cycle. Many economists label the new economic cycle as "high tech," because it incorporates new technologies into our society. In so labeling the new economic cycle, there is a tendency to overlook the importance that older, established industries will continue to play, although their significance will be somewhat lessened as time passes. Thus the label "postindustrial" is more appropriate than "high-tech" for the new economic cycle.

The economic problems that brought about the decline in the last cycle have since been recognized, and some corrective measures have begun to take effect. Original estimates of oil consumption increases and the resulting shortages projected have been revised as energy conservation has become of major importance to worldwide economic stability. As a result of conservation measures and an overall demand decrease, the price of oil has dropped significantly from its

4. The seven countries are Canada, France, Germany, Italy, Japan, the United Kingdom, and the United States: World Bank, *World Development Report*, pp. 11–13.

previous peak of thirty-five dollars per barrel, with even lower prices possibly on the way.[5] This reduction in oil demand was brought on by a number of things: reduction of nonessential uses of energy; increased use of advanced technology in engineering, design and production; and the introduction of sophisticated energy-management systems.

Another positive development has been the realization that an increase in real wages must be related to an increase in productivity. During the 1970s, real wages continued to grow, despite some drastic declines among many of the industrialized nations' aggregate productivity levels.[6] Although unemployment rates continued their dramatic rise, the 1980s were characterized by a new alignment between labor and management in an effort to bring real wages in line with productivity advances. By working together with labor, many companies facing bankruptcy were able to lower their break-even levels and stay competitive. Most notable in the United States is the Chrysler Corporation's comeback, nurtured in part by more favorable labor contracts.

Deeply variable currency valuations during the decade of the 1970s substantially hurt world trade. The drastic drop in the dollar caused many international investors to remove their funds from dollars and place them into other currencies, thus eliminating a key source of funds for U.S. capital markets. The weak dollar of the seventies also hurt those countries exporting to the United States by raising the price of their products to American consumers. That situation has since corrected itself. Statistics from the International Monetary Fund show that the dollar rose more than 32 percent in trade-weighted terms between January of 1981 and 1984. The dollar has increased in comparative value by almost 100 percent against four major European currencies since 1980.

The strength of the dollar and other encouraging factors have led to a resurgence in capital investment in the United States. The Organization for Economic Cooperation and Development (OECD) reported that gross fixed investment increased at an annual rate of 21 percent for the second half of

5. "New York Mercantile Exchange Spot Prices," *New York Times*, (February 25, 1985).
6. World Bank, *World Development Report*, p. 16.

1983.[7] Although the OECD expects the pace of investment increase in the United States to slow, the organization feels that the overall picture will improve.

Just as capital investment is a measure of confidence in the economic future, so is the consensus viewpoint of economists. An early 1984 survey conducted by *Business Week* magazine of twenty-seven leading economists representing various interests provided an optimistic outlook on economic growth for the economy, with little chance for downturn in the near future. The average forecasts of the economists show real GNP of the United States growing at the rate of 4.4 percent per year. The magazine also surveyed thirteen leading econometric services, which predicted real GNP growth of 4.7 percent per year and consumer price index growth of 5 percent per year.[8]

Although these predictions were more promising than those of previous years, economists were being cautious. In actuality, according to the Council of Economic Advisors, Gross National Product (GNP) rose at an annual rate of 5.88 percent in 1984, and the consumer price index rose 4 percent during the year.[9] These conservative economic forecasts for 1984 by those economists surveyed by *Business Week* indicate a somewhat unexpected strength in the economy that may be expected to continue through 1988. Expectations, however, must always be seasoned with some caution, even though the U.S. stock markets reached new highs in 1986. A number of negative factors could bring on an unexpected economic downturn.

The most pressing issue confronting the world economy is the potential default of payment of the debt of developing countries. This debt crisis would lose some of its importance if economic interdependence had not increased substantially in recent years. A world banking system has evolved using modern electronic technology. It has greatly accelerated cash flows between the various sectors of the world economy. Thus,

7. "Economic and Financial Indicators, 2," *The Economist* (July 14, 1984): 98; "Economic and Financial Indicators, 1," *The Economist* (August 18, 1984): 81.
8. "The Consensus: No Sign of a Slowdown Anytime Soon," *Business Week* (March 21, 1984): 7.
9. Council of Economic Advisors, *Economic Indicators: December 1984, A Report Prepared for the Joint Economic Committee* (Washington, D.C.: Government Printing Office, 1984), pp. 1, 23.

the developing countries' debt crisis has taken on global importance. The effect of this interdependency on the U.S. banking system can best be demonstrated by the fact that "foreign borrowers now account for half or more of the total loans of many large U.S. banks."[10]

What has precipitated the current debt crisis of developing nations? Among other things the decade of the 1970s brought quickly rising oil prices as a result of the oil embargo of 1973. During those times, nations could be classified into two groups: those who produced oil and those who did not. In an effort to continue development, those non-oil-producing nations borrowed huge amounts of capital to pay for their energy and investment needs. Moreover, the oil-producing nations increased their capital investment in petroleum plant and production. As the prices of oil continued to increase, so did the need for the importing countries to borrow. This vicious cycle of debt rollover became known as "loan recycling."

Developing countries that also produced oil, such as Mexico, found their credit lines expanded once the oil price run-up began. Some of these borrowed on the assumption that oil prices and oil demand would continue their fast increase. When the oil glut began in 1981, causing the subsequent decline of oil prices, these developing countries found the income from their oil exports drastically reduced and with it their capacity to service their debt.

Although the strength of the dollar may be viewed as a positive development in some respects, a strong dollar has intensified the debt crisis. With exchange rates adversely affecting the actual amount of the payments that these countries must make to U.S. banks (it is estimated that the nine largest U.S. banks have lent approximately 130 percent of their equity to Mexico, Brazil, and Argentina alone), a strong dollar has forced greater austerity measures on budgets already strained.[11]

National budgets and public spending have also received much attention in the United States. The World Bank report places the figures into historical perspective:

10. Trend Analysis Program, American Council of Life Insurance, "Five Potential Crises," *The Futurist* (April, 1984): 15.
11. Ibid., p. 16.

— Industrial countries saw a rise in public spending from 29.3 percent of GDP in 1961 to 40.9 percent in 1981.
— Among the seven major industrial countries, spending on education, health care, income maintenance, welfare and social security rose from 10.5 percent of GNP in 1954 to 23.4 percent of GNP in 1980.
— To help cover the costs of this expansion, taxes rose from 28.7 percent of GDP in 1961 to 37.5 percent in 1981.[12]

The World Bank also explains that "the significance of the general rise in public sector deficits is controversial, in part because of the difficulty of separating the effects of business cycles and inflation from those of structural trends in these deficits. It can be argued that the deficits may sometimes have acted as a valuable support for demand during a period of recession. It is undeniable, however, that depending on the method of financing, deficits have caused difficulty in some countries at particular times."[13]

These two situations, the debt crisis and government spending, clearly present the biggest problems that the world economy faces in the short term. If the recovery stage of the post-industrial economic cycle is to continue, certain adjustments must be made. First, a strong review of lending practices to developing nations must be implemented. This review should set criteria for lending as well as clearly define the roles of our international banking institutions, that is, the International Monetary Fund (IMF) and the World Bank. The current austerity measures implemented by the IMF on the developing countries with massive debt problems must be carried out even though short-term economic stagnation might occur. Another possible tactic would be to restructure some of the existing debt to more reasonable terms, even though this might cut into the profits of those lending institutions involved. Both options are already under review by bankers and public policymakers.

The future of the economic recovery stage in the United States and some other industrialized nations depends to a large extent on how governments handle their budget deficits. As

12. World Bank, *World Development Report*, p. 16.
13. Ibid.

government spending continues to grow and consume more of the GDP each year, leaving less for the private sector to invest, one thing becomes clear: if the world economy is to continue its recent growth, government spending must be reduced to allow the private sector more capital to invest. Although this may seem to fall into the realm of common sense, in reality, economists feel there is little chance of reducing government spending in the near term. Since modern governments have historically found it difficult to control their spending proclivities, it is most probable that the slowdown in budget growth will be gradual, with the difference made up by some form of tax increase. Although the debt crisis and government spending are critical elements in determining the growth or stagnation of the postindustrial world order, perhaps even more basic is an analysis of the supply of raw materials and resources necessary to sustain the new order.

World Resources

Any study attempting to predict future economic trends must focus on the availability of various important resources. Economic systems allow for the transfer of natural resources from a raw material state with little utility to a finished product with relatively high utility, that is, the value added by manufacturing. Thus, economic systems provide the method for creating wealth or value from raw materials. High rates of consumption of some of the world's resources (primarily oil) have focused attention on the disturbing fact that the earth's resources are finite. Many analysts began to inquire into the future availability of important resources and to examine their potential effect on the quality of life of future generations. Studies have produced a variety of findings and much debate.

Two of the most influential reports in the last decade take a decidedly different view of the future of the world's resources and the possibilities of sustained growth. The first, *The Global 2000 Report to the President*, was conducted at the request of President Jimmy Carter and was prepared by the Council on Environmental Quality and the Department of State. The report, published in 1980 (with revisions in 1982), used data collected from various U.S. government agencies together with global models to project environmental, resource, and population developments through the year 2000. The study presented disturbing conclusions and was pessimistic in its view of the quality of life for future generations worldwide.

The other report to have great influence in this field is *The Resourceful Earth*. Often cited as "a response to Global 2000," the study was organized by Herman Kahn and Julian Simon and includes the work of many noted scholars, authors, scientists, and economists. *The Resourceful Earth* presents a decidedly different perspective of global conditions in the year 2000, with a "cautiously optimistic" view.

The *Global 2000* report begins with the following view:

> If major trends continue, the world in 2000 will be more crowded, more polluted, less stable ecologically, and more vulnerable to disruption than the world we live in now. Serious stresses involving population, resources, and environment are clearly visible ahead. Despite greater material output, the world's people will be poorer in many ways than they are today.
>
> For hundreds of millions of the desperately poor, the outlook for food and other necessities of life will be no better. For many, it will be worse. Barring revolutionary advances in technology, life for most people on earth will be more precarious in 2000 than it is now—unless the nations of the world act decisively to alter current trends.[14]

The Resourceful Earth, however, challenges the findings of *Global 2000* by rewording the foregoing text to produce this statement:

> If present trends continue, the world in 2000 will be *less crowded* (though more populated), *less vulnerable to resource-supply disruption* than the world we live in now. Stresses involving population, resources, and environment *will be less in the future than now.* . . . The world's people will be *richer* in most ways than they are today. . . . The outlook for food and other necessities of

14. Council on Environmental Quality and the Department of State, *The Global 2000 Report to the President*, vol. I (Washington, D.C.: Government Printing Office, 1982), p. 1, hereafter *The Global 2000 Report*.

life will be *better*. . . . life for most people on earth will be *less precarious* economically than it is now.[15]

Why such a variance of opinion between *The Global 2000 Report* and *The Resourceful Earth?* The reason has a great deal to do with the opinions of those conducting the study. These opinions tend to influence the approaches and methods used to gather and analyze data. Thus *Global 2000* analysts were concerned that the world faced "enormous, urgent, and complex problems" in the decades immediately ahead. They counseled prompt and vigorous changes in public attitudes and policy before the problems became unmanageable. "If decisions are delayed until the problems become worse, options for effective action will be sorely reduced," the analysts advised.[16]

On the other hand, *The Resourceful Earth* authors expressed confidence in the likelihood of continuing improvement in humankind's economic lot. Improvement would not be without pitfalls and peril, however. Local problems, pollution, climatic changes, and population pressures would occur. But the resilience of a well-functioning economic and social system would provide the means and flexibility to overcome those problems. Moreover, the "solutions usually leave us better off than if the problem had never arisen; that is the great lesson to be learned from human history."[17]

The divergent reports do provide two interesting scenarios of the future that are important projections of the world economic order. It is useful to examine these projections in the light of population trends and resource and environmental developments.

Population Trends

The Global 2000 Report estimates world population growth at 1.8 percent annually until the year 2000. This would produce a 55 percent increase in world population, from 4.1 billion people in 1975 to 6.35 billion in the year 2000. Ninety-two

15. Julian Simon and Herman Kahn, eds. *The Resourceful Earth* (Oxford: Basil Blackwell, 1981), p. 1, original emphasis.
16. *The Global 2000 Report*, p. 5.
17. Simon and Kahn, eds., *The Resourceful Earth*, p. 3.

percent of the world's population growth is expected to occur in the less-developed countries, that is, in those countries least equipped to handle it. The demographic composition of the world's populations will shift dramatically to a more youthful population in the less-developed countries, with perhaps a trend toward older median ages in the wealthier countries, where lengthening life expectancy and lower birth rates create more mature populations.[18]

Populations will shift in less-developed countries from rural areas to large urban areas. Cities such as Bombay and Calcutta are expected to reach 19 million-plus, with Mexico City reaching an astounding 31.6 million persons by the year 2000. The expected rapid urban growth will put extreme pressure on sanitation, water supplies, health care, food, shelter, and jobs. Urban services, water, electricity, sanitation, and transportation and communication facilities will have to be expanded by two-thirds just to stay even with 1975 per capita use. Slums and shantytowns, where sanitation and services are minimal or nonexistent, are expected to proliferate.[19] It is a grim outlook for improving the quality of life for the world's aggregate populations.

A contrasting perspective is developed in *The Resourceful Earth*. Mark Perlman, a University of Pittsburgh professor of economics, drafted the section of the study relating to population trends and was very critical of the *Global 2000* conclusions. He argues that the "terrifying projection" for the year 2000 had little meaning. The projections, he says, had already proved off the mark. Perlman explains that Samuel Baum, who wrote the population section of the *Global 2000* report, changed his figures two years after the report was released to an estimate of 6.22 billion total world population in the year 2000, rather than the 6.35 billion originally estimated. Although the figure differential seems relatively small, the point is, Perlman notes, that the projections had to be changed at all after only two years. By 1984 the rate of growth of the world's population had already fallen below 1.8 percent per year, which the *Global 2000 Report* projected would not occur until the year 2000.[20]

18. *The Global 2000 Report*, p. 9.
19. Ibid.
20. Simon and Kahn, eds., *The Resourceful Earth*, pp. 52–53.

Perlman points to the historical inaccuracies of population predictions by U.S. forecasters as grounds for viewing the findings of the *Global 2000 Report* with skepticism. Noting that fertility and mortality rates are the major factors considered when predicting future population levels, he argues that fertility rates fluctuate too dramatically and are influenced by too many complex social interactions for there to be great confidence afforded forecasters using such predictions.

The more important difference between the two positions is the interpretation of what the impact of their numbers will have on the quality of life. *The Resourceful Earth,* although disagreeing with the alarming statistics forecast in the population predictions of *Global 2000,* concedes that there will be a substantial (but manageable) growth in the aggregate population. Perlman finds no empirical data that indicate a negative correlation between the rate of population growth and the quality of life.[21] Historically, more people does not mean a decline in living standards. The presumption that more people mean fewer natural resources per capita does not necessarily follow.

Natural Resources and the Environment

The natural resources that most significantly affect human welfare are foods (agricultural and marine), forests, nonfuel minerals, water, and energy. The future management of these resources will have a major impact on the standard of living of the world's population and its environment. A brief examination of the resources by category provides some insight into the potential supplies for future generations.

Foods

Thomas Malthus, an eighteenth-century British economist, is one of the most famous "futurists." He argued that the world's population grows at a geometric rate, but food production increases only at an arithmetic rate. Humankind, he

---

21. Ibid. p. 62. Note Perlman's reference to three demographic studies researching the possible correlation between the population growth rate and per capita income growth rate.

posed, could only expect subsistence levels of existence, interposed by recurring famine, starvation, and depopulation. Certainly the search for food has been humanity's most persistent endeavor. On occasion there have been serious failures and famine. Are starvation and want inevitable? Will there never be enough to go around? And by definition, as Malthus suggested, whenever there *are* ample supplies of foodstuffs, will there be a resulting overproduction of the species, leading inevitably to scarcity, famine, and depopulation? In the year 2000 will population expansion have exceeded the capacity of the earth to produce enough foodstuffs?

The Global 2000 Report projects food production to increase at an annual rate of 2.2 percent between 1970 and 2000. This translates into an overall increase of 90 percent of the food supply, which is favorable and positive compared to projected increases in population. Although this is an encouraging statistic, *Global 2000* predicts problems in various geographic locations that already have serious food shortages.

Less-developed countries as a group averaged only 94 percent of the minimum calorie intake requirements during the 1970s, according to the United Nations Food and Agriculture Organization (FAO). Some regions and the economically disadvantaged in those areas received substantially less than the average calorie intake reported. Furthermore, projected food production increases require greater use of fertilizers and pesticide applications, which means an increased dependency on petroleum products. The *Global 2000* study argues that the added costs associated with these petroleum products will prohibit their use in many of the lesser-developed countries, thus requiring an increased amount of imported food subsidies from the major food-producing countries, principally the United States.[22]

Another problem explored by *Global 2000* concerns the amount of fertile land that will be suitable for production. Because most fertile land is already in use, and given pressures on that land coming from urban expansion and alternative uses, the world is expected to add little to the lands in cultivation. The result, the analysts projected, will be an increase in the number of persons supported by one unit of land from

22. *The Global 2000 Report*, p. 17.

the 1970 level of 2.6 people per unit to 4.0 people per unit by the year 2000, and thus, food shortages.

The *Global 2000* study projects additional food shortages deriving from declining fish catches. Fish harvests in the year 2000 are expected to be approximately the same as in 1980, and even these supplies will be threatened by growing pollution problems. In summary, "Harvest of traditional fisheries are not likely to increase on a sustained basis, and indeed to maintain them will take good management and improved protection of the marine environment."[23] The projection is reminiscent of one made by Paul Erlich in 1969. He predicted that by 1977 the world fish catch would decline to thirty million metric tons and lead to the starvation of fifty million additional people per year. In actuality, the world fish catch in 1977 was 73 million tons, more than double the predicted levels.

The Resourceful Earth refutes the argument that the worldwide supply of foodstuffs (agricultural and marine) will result in shortages in regional areas and create a malnourished Third World underclass. The main thrust of the report's response centers on the evolution of an increasingly efficient world food market. This production and distribution system, the report states, has only recently been implemented on a wide scale, and increases in efficiency will occur as time passes. Access to food now depends primarily on financial status, and not on availability. Thus the problem is essentially one of distribution rather than production.

The world agricultural distribution system has brought about improvements in food supplies per capita in low-income countries, decreases in real prices of some major sources of nutrition (grains), and has made available on a large scale to developing countries the resources needed to increase the per capita food production level.[24] What this means is that food consumption per person has increased over the last thirty years, with even the lowest-income countries improving their situations. Food distributions, bad crops, and famine have by no means been eliminated, however.

There are problems. Africa has had a per capita decline in production. The Soviet Union has intermittently had poor

23. Ibid., p. 23.
24. Simon and Kahn, eds., *The Resourceful Earth*, p. 68.

wheat harvests. Peru has experienced a sharp drop in its fish catch. Many, if not most, countries have experienced a loss or decline in the supply of certain crops. But in some situations the cause has nothing to do with production capability. In Africa, for example, governmental mismanagement has contributed to the famines. The Peruvian marine catch has returned to approximately normal levels, as has that of most fishing countries.[25] There is evidence that world food supplies can be sustained under growing population pressures if distribution is effectively managed and generally follows free-market forces without government overregulation.

Forests

The *Global 2000 Report* states that 90 percent of wood consumption in less-developed countries is used for essential heating and cooking, making it the primary source of energy for individual households. The report predicts that "both forest cover and growing stocks of commercial-size wood in the less developed regions (Latin America, Africa, Asia, and Oceania) will decline 40 percent by 2000."[26] Given a projection of continually rising petroleum prices, the depletion of forest fuels is particularly critical for the less-developed nations, which can ill afford the more expensive fuels. Deforestation, moreover, could have serious effects on watersheds and contribute to long-term ecological damage.

Resourceful Earth analysts believe that the 40 percent deforestation rate is far off the mark. First, some of the current deforestation is a result of clearing lands for agricultural and other uses, although the wood being harvested is coincidentally being used as a source of fuel. This, the report contends, is a natural process in developing countries and, in many respects, follows the same pattern the United States followed during earlier growth stages.

The United States faced a "timber crisis" at the turn of the century. We were cutting annually more timber than was being brought into production. New housing and commercial construction, cross-ties for the railroads, and fuel for stoves and factories consumed ever-greater quantities of timber. But

25. Ibid., p. 115.
26. *The Global 2000 Report*, p. 26.

within decades the "timber famine" had disappeared. Why? Because production increased, and, more important, new technology, including such mundane things as using more and better wood preservatives, completing the conversion to coal, gas, and electric fuel, and changing materials in construction from wood to concrete, steel, and glass, changed consumption patterns. Market forces overcame the crisis, even before it was recognized as a crisis by the public. In the less-developed and temperate regions, there is evidence today that overall forest production is increasing, with no serious deforestation problems occurring, and prospects for developing alternative fuel sources are good.[27]

Nonfuel Minerals

Both the *Global 2000* and the *Resourceful Earth* people agree that there will be no major worldwide shortages of those nonfuel minerals essential to industrial production, even though consumption is expected to double by the year 2000.[28] The reports differ somewhat in their analysis of regional consumption and production rates, as well as of the costs of various important minerals. We can conclude, however, that market forces should be able to manage nonfuel mineral resources effectively well into the next century.

Water

In contrast to the optimistic report on nonfuel minerals, the outlook for water resources is less promising. *Global 2000* predicts severe problems with the worldwide water supply. The reasons given are (1) an expected increase in world water consumption by at least 200 to 300 percent by the year 2000, (2) increased consumption in less-developed regions already experiencing difficulty due to huge population increases, (3) increased industrial use, (4) dramatic increases in the costs involved in reducing larger amounts of usable water from a limited supply, and (5) losses in the overall supply of

27. Simon and Kahn, eds., *The Resourceful Earth*, pp. 128–29; Charles Maurice and Charles W. Smithson, *The Doomsday Myth* (Stanford, Calif.: Stanford University, Hoover Institution Press, 1984), pp. 45–59.

28. *The Global 2000 Report*, p. 27; Simon and Kahn, eds., *The Resourceful Earth*, pp. 128–29.

water and severe regional shortages due to environmental changes.[29]

The Resourceful Earth report maintains that many of the problems outlined by *Global 2000* are not as severe as described and can be effectively managed. Positive aspects listed in this more optimistic perspective are (1) improvement in world-wide understanding of the various factors affecting water resources, (2) increased concern in the private sector and more widespread and better use of conservation techniques, (3) improvement in environmental protection standards on a regional basis, and (4) a better understanding of the world's freshwater resources by using more complete and accurate data.[30] The main conclusion is that the predictions of the *Global 2000 Report* do not take into consideration the probability of the world's increasing its capacity to manage effectively its freshwater resources.

Energy

The Global 2000 Report projects that the energy situation will remain weak, with oil continuing as the primary energy source. Although alternative energy sources will be more heavily utilized, they will remain minor in the overall picture. Energy supplies and costs in less-developed countries will become much worse, with many having to burn animal waste to fill personal heating and cooking needs. The costs involved in producing energy sources will increase substantially, according to *Global 2000,* with oil prices estimated to increase by 65 percent by 1990.[31]

The energy environment, however, has changed significantly since the appearance of the report. In 1982, for example, the average cost of a barrel of imported crude fell from $37.50 to $33.72, and $15 per barrel oil has since become a reality. By the time the *Resourceful Earth* report appeared in 1984, the energy crisis seemed to have been substantially resolved, and the OPEC cartel was near collapse. Nevertheless, a special report of the U.S. Geological Survey on world petroleum

29. *The Global 2000 Report,* p. 26.
30. Simon and Kahn, eds., *The Resourceful Earth,* p. 259.
31. *The Global 2000 Report,* p. 27.

resources in 1985 cautioned that the discoveries of new oil appeared to be on a permanent decline and that the Middle East would continue to monopolize the world's petroleum supplies.

The Resourceful Earth analysis agrees with *Global 2000* that overall energy use will indeed increase by the year 2000, but the increase will be less dramatic because of increased energy efficiency and the greater use of nonoil energy sources. The report proposes that oil consumption in developed countries will decrease substantially, forcing prices to drop. The United States, for example, imported less than 30 percent of its petroleum in 1984, as compared to about 50 percent in 1979. Alternative energy sources such as nuclear fission and fusion energy are expected to become increasingly important. *Resourceful Earth* people believe that there are new and untapped energy sources in relatively unlimited amounts that only require the technology to be developed. The overall result, concludes the report, will be a greater choice of energy sources and declining consumer costs.

Why should there be two such divergent forecasts for the future? Part of the explanation is, of course, that the more recent *Resourceful Earth* report had access to new and, in the case of petroleum, distinctly different data. The big difference, however, seems to be largely attitudinal. The variation in the two reports is largely based on the expectations of the degree to which people can effect changes in managing the world's resources. *The Global 2000* Report views humans in a static management role, with "environment" and natural resources being the active or controlling factor. Conversely, the *Resourceful Earth* philosophy seems to be based on the perception that there has been a historical pattern of improvement in the quality of life on earth, and there is no reason to think that pattern will change.

The Human Factor:
Changing Work Patterns

One of the most impressive changes occurring in the postindustrial society is the ways in which we work. Indeed, the very definition of work is changing from the traditional perception of work as having to do with manual labor or involved in the creation or manufacture of material products to the concept of work as having to do with ideas, information, and knowledge. The older forms of work are those things increasingly done by robots and in automated factories where little human labor is involved.

Many individuals are already experiencing dramatic shifts in employment opportunities. Those who are supported by a traditional "smokestack" industrial base are being forced to reassess their future. This is especially true of people within specific regions of the United States, such as the Northeast and the Midwest, and in Western Europe in the industrial areas of the United Kingdom, France, and Germany, where labor costs remain high compared with those in developing countries. Another factor is the introduction of sophisticated high-technology systems, such as robotics, which have reduced the need for traditional human labor in manufacturing processes. Many predict that this trend of "deindustrialization" will continue at an increased rate. Marvin Cetron, president of Forecasting International and the author of several books on the subject, predicts major changes in the U.S. job market: "Manufacturing will provide only 11% of the jobs in the year 2000, down from 28% in 1980. Jobs related to agriculture will drop from 4% to 3%. The turn of the century will find the remaining 86% of the work force in the service sector, up from 68% in 1980. Of the service-sector jobs, half will relate to information collection, management and dissemination."[32] John Naisbitt, author of the best-seller *Megatrends*, says that most Americans already spend their time creating, processing or distributing information.[33]

In addition, the information revolution has led to an entrepreneurial explosion in the United States. In 1950, new businesses were being created at the rate of 93,000 a year, and in 1983 the rate was more than 600,000 a year. Of the nine million people added to the labor force between 1976 and 1983, Naisbitt estimates that six million were employed in businesses that had been in existence for four years or less. MIT's

32. Marvin Cetron, "Getting Ready for the Jobs of the Future," *The Futurist* (June, 1983): 15.
33. John Naisbitt, *Megatrends: Ten New Directions Transforming Our Lives* (New York: Warner Books, 1982), p. 14.

David Birch explains that Americans are going out of the manufacturing business and into the thinking business.[34]

If predictions such as these prove true, where will the production of manufactured goods and the resulting jobs associated be located? It is true that increased productivity will account for some of the reductions in industrial employment in the United States and other industrialized nations, but the major cause of deindustrialization in these regions will be the movement of production facilities to developing countries, which is already occurring. Substantially lower labor costs together with generally lower tax rates have tempted many industries to move production facilities to these areas. Evidence of this can be seen in the growth rates of selected developing nations as compared to those of the more industrialized nations. The GDP of the industrial nations grew at an annual rate of 2.8 percent between 1973 and 1979 and developing countries enjoyed a 5.2 percent annual rise over the same period. In particular, the growth rate of GDP in the East Asia and the Pacific region grew at an annual rate of 8.6 percent during the same period, and many analysts predict continued growth and increased industrialization for the region in the near term.[35]

The loss of manufacturing jobs in industrialized economies has caused "structural unemployment" and has left many to wonder where tomorrow's jobs will come from. Most analysts concur that there will be continued increases in service-sector job opportunities to replace many of those displaced by structural unemployment. But these same analysts caution that this shift will require a massive retraining of the current work force to maximize future employment opportunities. Cetron predicts that the United States will see significant growth in the following existing job areas within the decade: Data processing machine mechanics, 157.1 percent growth; paralegal personnel, 143.0; computer systems analysts, 112.4; midwives, 110.0; computer operators, 91.7; office machine service technicians, 86.7; tax preparers, 77.9; computer programmers, 77.2; aero-astronautic engineers, 74.8; employment

34. Naisbitt, *Megatrends*, p. 16; David L. Birch, "Who Creates Jobs?" *The Public Interest* (Fall, 1981): 3–14.
35. World Bank, *World Development Report*, p. 11.

interviewers, 72.0; fast food restaurant workers, 69.4; childcare attendants, 66.5; veterinarians, 66.1; and chefs, 55.0.[36]

Cetron also lists new occupations that will arise due to the introduction and utilization of advanced technology in areas as diverse as energy, robotics, and medicine. All of these jobs will require specific technical expertise and, as a result, place greater importance on the quality of educational and vocational programs. The retraining process of those displaced workers must be widespread if economies are to continue to function efficiently. Table 1 identifies those relatively new or nonexisting employment areas that will absorb increasing portions of the work force in the decades ahead, and the predicted employment levels by the close of the 1980s.

Table 1   Postindustrial Employment Opportunities

Field	Occupation	Description	No. of Jobs in U.S. by 1990
Energy	Energy technician	Manage new energy sources	650,000
	Automotive fuel cell technician	Service fuel cells for vehicles and stationary operation	250,000
	Energy auditor	Use computers and infrared monitoring systems to conserve energy for home, business, and industrial complexes	180,000
Medical	Bionic-medical technician	Service bionic appendages and sensory-enhancing devices	200,000
	On-line emergency medical technician	Perform paramedical and support functions	400,000
	Geriatric social worker	Aid the aging population	700,000
	Nuclear medicine technologist	Work with radioisotopes to produce medicines for diagnostics	75,000
	Dialysis technologist	Operate new generation of dialysis machines	30,000
	CAT technician	Install, maintain, and operate CAT-scanning devices	45,000

36. Cetron, "Getting Ready," p. 17.

Table 1 — *Continued*

Field	Occupation	Description	No. of Jobs in U.S. by 1990
	PET technician	Install, maintain, and operate PET-scanning devices	165,000
	Genetic engineering technician	Develop genetically engineered materials for use in pharmaceuticals, industry, and agriculture	250,000
Industrial	Industrial laser process technician	Monitor and maintain laser production	600,000
	Industrial robot product technician	Monitor and maintain as well as coordinate robots into manufacturing process	800,000
	Materials utilization technician	Develop use of new materials (synthetics) in production process	400,000
	Holographic inspection specialist	Service and monitor automated systems that use fiberoptic sensors	200,000
Waste Management	Hazardous waste management technician	Meet demand for environmental safety	300,000
Construction	House rehabilitation technician	Service prefabricated modular homes using radically new construction techniques	500,000
Computers	Computer-assisted design technician	Product design and structural tests by computer	300,000
	Computer-assisted graphics technician	Design graphics for new products, with new forms and dimensions	150,000
	Computer-assisted manufacturing	Service and monitor computer-operated manufacturing system	300,000
	Computer vocational training technician	Instruct and develop courses and materials for computer-assisted training courses	300,000

Source: Marvin Cetron, "Getting Ready for the Jobs of the Future," *The Futurist* (June, 1983).

Just as the Industrial Revolution expanded the number of types of jobs and careers, the postindustrial era will see a change, most experts believe, as dramatic as the transformation of the Middle Ages to the Renaissance to the Industrial Revolution. S. Norman Feingold, president of the National Career and Counseling Service, explains that new occupations and careers emerge all the time. The elevator operator, the bowling pin setter, the milkman, and the harness maker have gone into oblivion, and in their place have come countless new occupations. The information industry offers the opportunity for the proliferation of new careers, because information is a limitless resource. Unlike finite industrial resources such as oil, ore, and iron, there is an inexhaustible supply of knowledge, concepts, and ideas."[37]

At present, the information sector represents an estimated 50 percent of the work force in industrialized nations. Several leading futurists at the World Future Society 1983 General Assembly predicted that "71% of the labor force in industrialized countries will work in the information and communications sector of the economy by the year 2000."[38]

As employment opportunities shift from manufacturing into these new areas, the effects on life-styles in industrialized nations will be dramatic. Greater technical training and emphasis on access to information will require workers to spend more time educating themselves with a host of new technologies that will become available. As we move toward the year 2000, major changes will occur in the workplace and at home. Alvin Toffler, for example, expects to see millions of jobs swept out of the factories and offices back to where they came from before the Industrial Revolution—the home.[39]

The importance of communication links grows as employment shifts from manufacturing to service and information-processing jobs. Individuals will find greater flexibility in their work habits and workplaces. "Homesteading" or "teleworking" will become more commonplace.

Teleworking allows an individual to work at home or at a more convenient work site than the office by using various

37. Norman Feingold, "Emerging Careers: Occupations for Post-Industrial Society," *The Futurist* (February, 1984): 9.
38. Cetron, "Getting Ready," p. 35.
39. Toffler, *The Third Wave*, p. 205.

communication links to transfer information. It is estimated that by the year 2000 one-third of the work force in industrialized nations will be involved in teleworking, and half of the managers will use electronic work stations to perform some of their tasks.[40] The result should be greater efficiencies or economies of labor. For example, there will be savings in time and travel costs. Studying 2,048 insurance company employees in Los Angeles, the Nilles group found that each person, on average, traveled 21.4 miles a day to and from work. The higher up the managerial scale, the longer the commute, with top executives averaging 33.2 miles. All together, these workers drove 12.4 million miles each year to get to work, using up nearly fifty years' worth of potential working hours to do so.[41] At 1974 prices, this cost twenty-two cents per mile, or a total of $2.73 million. Downtown workers received an average of $520 more pay per year than those employees working in dispersed locations, which amounted to a company subsidy of travel costs. In addition, the company provided parking spaces and other expensive services that were not provided at less-central locations. It was estimated that commuting expenses cost the company what three hundred additional employees would have cost—or a corresponding loss of potential profit.[42]

The higher cost of central business district properties, parking, and services argues for disbursed employment. Teleworking offers the company the opportunity to reduce real capital investment in physical space, which is essentially nonproductive, and to invest in people, who are productive. It also offers the possibility of expanding the labor pool by making it possible for the handicapped to attain full-time employment within the home, and it offers the possibility for mothers with small children to remain in the labor force.[43] Greater flexibility in working hours should also increase the productivity of labor. Flextime is a relatively new innovation that allows employees to choose their own work hours. It began in West Germany in 1965, when it was recommended as a way to bring more mothers into the job market.

40. Cetron, "Getting Ready," p. 35.
41. Toffler, *The Third Wave*, pp. 198–200.
42. Ibid.
43. Ibid., pp. 246–47, 251–52.

Flextime, of course, is something the teleworker would also have, but neither flextime or teleworking will eliminate the more traditional or central city workplace. Many workers will not want to stay at home and work in their "electronic cottage," even if they can. People want to be with people. Interpersonal contact, management supervision, support from co-workers in problem-solving situations, and social interaction and pleasure are components of the traditional workplace. Teleworking and flextime will, however, provide an important and economically efficient supplement to the traditional work time and place. It is already a feature of the postindustrial society and is prominent in such professional work activities as laboratories and universities.

The reality is that the postindustrial society is having a distinct impact on the way we work, how we work, and where we work. This affects our life-style and our philosophy of life. Our political, religious, social, and intellectual lives are inextricably tied to our economic welfare, both as individuals and as a nation. Will this new work-world bring us prosperity and progress? Will it offer only subsistence, at best? Or is the greater likelihood that our economic future will be one of dislocation and greater poverty?

What the Future Probably Holds

Predicting economic growth or decline for a particular country, region, or for the world, is a precarious endeavor. The data used to analyze economies change, often rapidly, and many of the factors accounting for the change remain obscure. Unforeseen developments such as war or natural disaster can topple a government or bring a sound economy to its knees. The destructive earthquake in Mexico City in September, 1985, has had economic repercussions that are still unfolding. How then can one reasonably approach the complicated problem of predicting the future of the world's economy?

It is necessary to attempt an understanding of the primary factors that determine the growth pattern of an economic cycle. By understanding these factors, it is possible to develop a general overview of where the economy is headed with respect to long-term trends. These trends or cyclical projections, although not specific in nature, tend to be more accurate and allow for corrections in response to unforeseen developments.

Primary factors behind the economic growth of the modern industrial cycle included petroleum, chemicals, and manufacturing. As the rate of growth in these dynamic areas of economic activity subsided, the economy entered a mature phase and then a state of decline. Under free-market pressures and opportunities, capital was gradually diverted from the slow-growth industries to the high-growth areas, which become the new primary factors in the next economic cycle. Thus information and communications systems, genetic engineering, space and services, with other new or developing industries, will constitute the leading edge of economic development in the next postindustrial economic cycle.

The possibilities of an extended period of worldwide economic growth remain good if current conditions in free-market countries remain reasonably stable. An important factor will be the degree to which governments involve themselves in the affairs of the private sector. The negative effects of large government spending programs and trade protection, or the nationalizing of private corporations to protect the inefficient, erode growth opportunities in the postindustrial cycle.

Remembering that we have constructed a model of an economic cycle patterned on the modern industrial cycle (and earlier cycles) and that the model contains four stages — recovery, expansion, maturity, and decline — how might we superimpose this model on the conditions or projections for economic development that we have thus far considered? Can we give our postindustrial cycle a more precise definition? Using dates, although admitting their fragility, might give us a sharper image.

The recovery period, lasting for the decade 1985–1995, will be a time of transition. Economic "growing pains" will cause the GNP of industrialized nations to grow at a lower rate. The growth rate will begin to accelerate as new industries supersede the old. Unemployment will remain a serious problem. New business formation and small enterpreneurs will create the bulk of new jobs in the industrialized nations.

Heavy, or traditional, manufacturing industries will shift to the developing nations. Areas of greatest activity will include East Asia, the Pacific nations (prominently Korea, Taiwan, and China), Central America and the Caribbean, and

Brazil and Argentina in South America. Although they could change, the trends in this direction are already well established. The total volume of manufactured goods will continue to increase in the industrialized nations and will still account for most of the world's manufactured product, but the industrial nations will experience a much slower rate of economic growth than will the developing nations. Petroleum will remain critical in the world economic order. There should be small advances toward agricultural self-sufficiency, with particular gains on the African continent, and a gradual slowdown of the rate of growth in the world's populations should continue.

The postindustrial expansion period could last for two decades, from 1995 to 2015, during which time the economic cycle would move into a period of high productivity and substantial economic growth. This period might be equated roughly to the economic prosperity of the 1912–1929 era, or the 1945–1965 modern industrial era. Unemployment problems will ease as nations and societies adjust to new developments and business structures. The introduction of new technologies into the workplace as well as into the home will become commonplace. New telecommunication and data systems will provide companies with enough information to compete on a global scale and facilitate world marketing systems. The multinational corporation will have largely displaced the traditional corporation in size and influence, and governments might be expected to be struggling to maintain a degree of regulation or control over them. These efforts could lead to greater intergovernmental cooperation along the lines of the European Common Market. Currency and financial transactions will occur at greater speeds as electronic banking interlocks many of the world's businesses, financial institutions, and governments.

As the world economy expands, the standard of living for those persons in underdeveloped nations will increase substantially. Although it is unlikely that malnutrition and hunger will cease to exist, the availability of new technologies, such as the genetic engineering of crops, better fertilizers, laser beam cultivation systems, and water management programs, should enhance agricultural production in many regions of the world.

Space will be the new frontier for private sector investment. Enterpreneurs and investors will be attracted to opportunities in space travel, manufacture, and commercial adventure— including the search for precious materials. Consumer demand will grow greater as the base of economic welfare broadens and individual income rises.

During the period of maturity, from approximately 2015 through 2025, the postindustrial cycle will climax and world market and new production capacities resulting from the now old technologies will slow, as will consumer demand. In these maturing markets, a thinning out among competitors will occur as corporations seek to survive. Management will become more conservative. New start-ups will become fewer and venture capital more scarce, or at least more selective. Manufacturing facilities in those countries once considered "developing" will begin to become obsolete. The introduction of new products will slow. Efficient corporate resource management will be a major business consideration.

The final phase, of decline (2025–2035), will be not unlike the era from 1975 to 1985. There will be increasing economic dislocation and uncertainty. "Consumerism" will be the by-word as companies compete fiercely to save their market share. Capital will be removed from those ventures that are not producing an acceptable return. Consolidations will occur, as they did in the closing days of the industrial era, as businesses merge to survive. There will be a repeat of some of the old patterns, such as a move of manufacturing or corporate entities to new and lesser-developed regions, in an effort to lower costs. Africa might well be the new host. Diversification will be a corporate rule. Unemployment will rise and production capacities will be underutilized. But it is likely that the seeds of the next economic cycle will be sown and already bearing fruit.

One might, of course, argue that all of this is both simplistic and overly optimistic. The model for future economic expectations is certainly fragile, a view through a dark looking glass. War, natural disaster, and certainly governmental intervention are quite likely. These occurrences are no more possible, however, than are countervailing possibilities, which could hasten the development of the postindustrial cycle, such as breakthroughs in energy technology especially derived from some space research station.

The fact is that the processes of change leading to the post-industrial era are already evident. The information and communications revolution is technologically complete and is becoming a commercial reality. Home computers, which provide access to a variety of information packages and systems, cable and satellite communications, television systems, laser communications, and new printing and photocopying processing techniques are revolutionizing the information system. The movement of traditional manufacturing plants to developing countries is occurring with astonishing speed. Employment patterns are changing. The manufacture of special crystals has already occurred in space, and vested private space ventures have already been a part of numerous satellite and shuttle cargoes. Given the finite resources of the earth, the growing populations, and the almost infinite possibilities that the postindustrial era might be sidetracked, should we expect a better future, one about the same, or one more desperate and grim?

Given humankind's remarkable survivability and social accomplishment, perhaps optimistic projections can be made with some confidence. Economists Charles Maurice and Charles W. Smithson argue in their recent book, *The Doomsday Book: 10,000 Years of Economic Crises,* that, since the marketplace has worked for the past ten thousand years to eliminate resource shortages, why should we expect that it will not work in the future? Similarly, Herman Kahn and John Phelps, with the Hudson Institute, suggest that, "barring serious bad luck or bad management," the prospects for achieving a broad-based and high level of worldwide affluence and "beneficient technology" are bright.[44]

Although projections and predictions may after a time be proven to be somewhat askew, it is rather important that society, just as the individual does, make projections and predictions. They become a part of personal and social aspirations. Those aspirations themselves become a dynamic fac-

---

44. Herman Kahn and John B. Phelps, "The Economic Present and Future," *The Futurist* (June, 1979): 202.

tor in social and economic development. As Kahn and Phelps explain, "our images of the economic future may substantially determine our progress toward that goal." People and nations need not be merely the victims of change, but should become the managers of change.

CHAPTER TWO

The Late, Great Society

Changes in family structure, in the role of women, and in the care and education of children, different immigration profiles, and changing demographic trends indicate that American society will be different in the future. Exactly how different, and in what ways, is a matter of speculation and reasoned projection.

Ours is a society in flux. Old certainties are being challenged while new values are in the process of development. New life-styles have clearly brought about greater personal freedom. Women and minorities have more closely approached economic and social equality. The "general welfare" has distinctly improved for most Americans since 1936. Our world is considerably different from that of fifty years ago in terms of material welfare, where we live, what we do, and what options or opportunities we have.

America is aging. Our average lifespan has increased almost a dozen years since 1935. In 1935, the teenager hardly existed as a dimension of American society. There were children and adults. At the peak of the modern industrial cycle, almost two decades after World War II, almost one-half of all Americans were under the age of twenty-five. Two decades later there are more Americans over the age of sixty-five than there are teenagers. By 2035 one in five persons will be over sixty-five.

We have closed an era of unparalleled expansion in the quantity and quality of life. There have also been adversities and losses. In our haste to move ahead, we have in some respects lost our past. We have become a disconnected or disassociated society. Our preoccupation with the present has been accompanied by a rejection of the past, and the result has been a certain drift or social mindlessness. Nevertheless, if one probes the whirlwinds of social change, certain trends and patterns suggest a remarkably clear perception of the dimensions of American society in the coming postindustrial era.

Will the family as the primary social unit survive the ravages of the past fifty years and the anticipated rigors of the next half century? What impact will the aging of America have on social structures and values? Can the women and present minorities in American society, particularly blacks, Hispanics, and Asians, anticipate improved opportunities or greater assimilation? Given the current dimensions of crime in America, will our persons and our property be safe in the society of the future?

On Crime and Punishment

The chances of being the victim of a violent crime have nearly tripled in the last twenty-five years, as has the possibility of being the victim of a serious crime such as burglary or theft. Fifty years ago the word *mugging* was not in most dictionaries. Violent crimes now touch more than 10 percent of U.S. households. If larceny is included, the number of households affected increases to 30 percent. According to the Federal Bureau of Investigation's "crime clock," one crime is committed every two seconds, one violent crime every twenty-four seconds, and one property crime every three seconds. One American is murdered every twenty-three minutes, one is raped every six minutes, and one assaulted every forty-nine seconds. In 1951, a New York City police force of more than nineteen thousand was asked to cope with 15,812 violent crimes. In 1982 a New York force of twenty-two thousand confronted 157,026 such crimes.[1]

Safety is becoming a big business everywhere. There are now twice as many private guards as there are sworn police officers. A December, 1983, Justice Department report declares

1. Allan C. Brownfeld, "Rule That Protects Criminals Leaves Us Less Safe," *New York Tribune* (December 17, 1983).

that Americans have a greater chance of becoming victims of violent crime than of being injured in an automobile accident. In 1983, violent crimes led to two million deaths. Injuries and financial losses for the year were more than ten billion dollars.[2]

Curiously, although crime has increased, the chance of a criminal's actually going to jail has declined. For every five hundred crimes, only 20 adults and 5 juveniles, on average, are sent to jail—a ratio of 20 to 1. Of some two million serious criminal cases filed each year, only one in five actually goes to trial. In New York State in 1980, of the 130,000 men and women arrested for felonies, only about 8,000 went to prison. Sociologists calculate that if the robbery rate in large cities continues to grow as it did between 1962 and 1974, by the year 2024 each man, woman, and child in a large city would be robbed by force or threat of force 2.3 times per year.[3]

Another concern to most Americans, and a by-product of the permissive society that ours has become, is the epidemic of drunk driving. In one decade, more than 250,000 Americans died at the hand of drunk drivers, more than four times the number of Americans killed during the ten years of fighting in the Vietnam War. One of every two Americans will be involved in an alcohol-related auto crash in his or her lifetime. John Mouldon, a research psychologist with the National Highway Safety Administration, believes that drunk driving has reached epidemic proportions because society has accepted drinking and driving as a normal part of daily life.[4]

The courts have often been lenient with drunk drivers, even with those who have killed. Practically every community has a case similar to that in Ixonia, Wisconsin, in which a previously convicted drunk driver struck and killed a child and was released with a suspended jail sentence and a light fine. In California a person having six previous convictions for drunk and reckless driving drove onto a sidewalk and killed a child waiting for the ice-cream man.[5]

The widespread use and tacit public approval of narcotics

2. Ibid.

3. Allan C. Brownfeld, "Crime: Facing Facts, Laying Myths to Rest," *Washington Times* (October 19, 1983).

4. Ibid.

5. Allan C. Brownfeld, "The War against Drunk Drivers," *Manchester (N.H.)*

have been equally devastating. Emergency room admissions related to cocaine use topped 13,000 in 1983. A survey of high-school students indicated that 16.5 percent used cocaine in 1984. According to the Drug Enforcement Administration, there are about 492,000 known heroin addicts in the United States, and about 4.4 metric tons of heroin are smuggled into the country each year. There are about 15 million cocaine users. It is estimated that 40 to 60 percent of all serious or violent crimes are drug-related. New York City recorded 1,882 drug-related homicides in 1981. As chief of detectives John T. Sullivan put it, "The use of drugs has become more extensive and pervasive, and when you have people selling drugs, you have guns, rivalries, rip-offs and, inevitably, violence."[6]

Americans are beginning to use drugs at an increasingly younger age. In 1971, a George Washington University study found that 6 percent of those in the twelve-to-seventeen-year-old age bracket smoked marijuana. In 1982, a similar survey indicated that the percentage had doubled. It is estimated that 64 percent of American young people will have tried an illegal drug before they finish high school, and more than a third will have used drugs other than marijuana. Thirty-three percent of Americans aged twelve and older have used marijuana, hallucinogens, cocaine, heroin, or psychotherapeutic drugs for nonmedical purposes.[7]

The pervasiveness of drug use among younger Americans has become increasingly clear, as events in the National Football League have shown. Don Reese, former defensive lineman for the New Orleans Saints, in June, 1982, stunned the sports world when he wrote that "cocaine arrived in my life with my first-round draft into the NFL in 1974. Eventually it took control and almost killed me. It may yet. Cocaine can be found in quantity throughout the NFL." The death of Leonard Bias, an outstanding basketball draft selection of the Boston Celtics, from cocaine intoxication in 1986 confirmed the growing use of cocaine into the 1980s.[8]

Union Leader (September 15, 1983); "The War against Drunk Drivers," *Newsweek* (September 13, 1982): 34–35.

6. "How Drugs Sap the Nation's Strength," *U.S. News and World Report* (May 16, 1983): 55.

7. Ibid.

8. Ibid.; "How Cocaine killed Leonard Bias," *Time* (July 7, 1986), p. 52.

A 1981 survey of U.S. military units in Europe showed that 16 percent of army personnel and almost a quarter of navy personnel used marijuana and hashish every day. After the May 26, 1981, crash of a Marine EA-6B aircraft on the deck of the *USS Nimitz*, autopsies performed on fourteen of the men killed showed that almost half showed signs of drug abuse and some had taken drugs shortly before death. In the six months prior to the crash, there were 124 cases of court-martial or nonjudicial punishment against the *Nimitz* crew for drug abuse.[9]

One reason for such widespread drug abuse is its increasing acceptability in certain elite groups in America, particularly those responsible for radio and television programming and the film industry. Dr. Richard Jessor, director of the Institute of Behavioral Science at the University of Colorado, declares that, "in a very short time, cultural patterns have changed dramatically. It is now normal for the majority of young people to have experience with a range of substances that was unavailable to previous generations."[10] Crime, drunk driving, and drug use — all of these are growing in an environment that is increasingly ambivalent about questions of what is right and what is wrong. Things that were once considered unacceptable and depraved are now accepted by many as routine.

Over ten years ago U.S. Surgeon General Jesse L. Steinfeld advised that the causal relation between television violence and antisocial behavior was sufficient to require immediate remedial action. The presidents of the three national networks agreed in a hearing before Congress. There was, however, little evidence of remedial action. The University of Pennsylvania's Annenberg School of Communications, which has studied television violence for almost two decades, reports that violent acts continue at the rate of about six per prime time hour in four out of five programs. Weekend children's programs have an even higher rate.[11]

One of the more insidious developments has been the growth in pornography, child pornography in particular. Child

9. Ibid.
10. Ibid.
11. Allan C. Brownfeld, "The Time Has Come to Clean Up American Television," *News World* (February 13, 1981).

pornography accounts for about one-fifth of the six-billion-dollar traffic in pornography. An overwhelming proportion is controlled by organized crime. As a moneymaker, the pornography racket ranks third behind drugs and gambling. The pornography business now includes some 20,000 bookstores, 400 magazines, and 780 movie houses, as well as mail-order businesses and cable television programming services that deal in obscene matter. *The Adult Business Report*, the trade newsletter of the pornography industry, boasts that there are three times the number of adult bookstores in the United States as there are McDonald's restaurants. As many as twenty million Americans are estimated to be regular readers of pornographic magazines and two million to three million Americans view pornographic movies each week. Videotapes of such films represent about 50 percent of the home movie market. There are at least 250 "kiddie porn" magazines on the market. Common themes include sadism, incest, child molestation, rape, and murder.[12]

It cannot be considered coincidental that the past decade has marked a rise in pornography sales and in crimes of sexual violence. Dr. Harold Voth, a senior psychiatrist at the Menninger Foundation, says that pornography is harmful. Contrary to what some people argue, "It suggests behavior to people who would never have thought of it in the first place," and it certainly suggests less civilized behavior than the accepted norm. A University of Wisconsin study completed in 1983 concluded that even "normal" men, prescreened college students, were changed by their exposure to pornography. After ten hours of viewing, "the men were less likely to convict in a rape trial, less likely to see injury to the victim, more likely to see the victim as responsible."[13]

In May, 1982, the National Institute of Mental Health issued a report summarizing more than twenty-five hundred studies in the last decade on television's influence on behavior. Evidence from the studies, with more than one hundred thousand subjects, overwhelmingly demonstrates that vio-

12. Allan C. Brownfeld, "Top Politicians Block or Ignore Measure to Curb Pornography," syndicated column distributed by Free Press International News Service, February 20, 1984.
13. Ibid.

lence on television does lead to aggressive behavior. According to the 1982 Nielsen Report, the average American family viewed television for 49.5 hours each week. The typical youngster graduating from high school will have spent almost twice as much time watching television as in the classroom. The youth will have witnessed about 150,000 violent episodes, including about 25,000 deaths. Saturday morning children's television offers about 25 violent acts each hour, and commercials have a rate of violence about three times that of the programs. Excessive television viewing seems to alter conceptions of social reality among children and adolescents and encourages an exaggerated sense of danger and mistrust.[14]

Television's treatment of sex seems to have similar pervasive influences. Fred MacMurray, star of a television series that ran for about twelve years, comments, "There doesn't seem to be anything you can't do on t.v. anymore—violence, sex, prostitution. There's nothing sacred or taboo." Kids get so used to violence and death on television, he says, that they could be unaffected when they see it in real life.[15] Despite better health care, food, and leisure-time opportunities, it is not so easy for the young to grow into mature and responsible adults.

Child abuse has become a serious social problem. Since 1900 the divorce rate has risen 700 percent. Except for a brief slowdown in 1977, it has increased each year since 1966, as have the absolute numbers of divorces. Since 1975, more than one million couples have divorced annually, with a record 1,182,000 marriages ending in divorce in 1980. For a time it appeared that more couples were getting unmarried than were getting married. Almost 50 percent of marriages end in divorce in the United States, compared with 17 percent in Japan, 9 percent in West Germany, 22 percent in France, 36 percent in Great Britain, and 4 percent in Italy.[16]

It is estimated that one million children annually are involved in divorce cases and thirteen million children under the age of eighteen are living in households with only one parent. More than half the nation's married women are now

14. Ibid.
15. "Number of Divorces Reached Record in 1981," *New York Times* (February 2, 1984).
16. Ibid.

employed outside the home, and it is estimated that Americans spend less time with their children than do parents in almost any other country.[17]

Although many children live in broken homes, many have never had two parents present. Illegitimate births increased so rapidly in the 1970s that 17 percent of U.S. babies, one out of every six, were born out of wedlock. In 1979, the last year for which statistics were tabulated, an estimated 597,000 illegitimate babies were born, up 50 percent since 1970. Among blacks in the United States, 55 percent of the children were born out of wedlock into female-headed homes, compared with an estimated 15 percent in 1940.[18]

There is evidence that ours is becoming a society that is indifferent, if not hostile, to children. Studies conducted in Houston, New York City, Phoenix, and Washington, D.C. suggest that one of every three urban children under the age of eighteen is a "latchkey" child, that is, a child left to do for himself or herself while parents are at work. Some are painfully young to be left alone.

Aggravating the situation is the fact that many fathers have abandoned all responsibility for their children. A study by the U.S. Census Bureau indicates that as of spring, 1982, 8.4 million women were living with a child under twenty-one years of age whose father was not living in the household. Fifty-nine percent, or about 5 million of the women, had been awarded child-support payments, but in 1981 only 47 percent of those who were due payments received the full amount. Many received nothing.[19]

The breakdown of the traditional family is in part responsible for the rising number of child abuse cases being reported. In part, the number results from the growing level of consciousness of child abuse by the public and the medical profession. In 1976, the American Humane Association found that 413,000 cases of child abuse had been reported to state and local authorities that year. By 1981, the count had more than

17. Marlene Aig, "Divorce: Some Kids Hide Hurt for Years," *Washington Times* (June 22, 1983).

18. Ibid.

19. "Family Unit Threatened by Rising Illegitimacy," *Washington Times* (June 22, 1983); Allan C. Brownfeld, "The Shocking Rise of Child Abuse and What It Says about Society," *Anaheim (Calif.) Bulletin* (December 31, 1982).

doubled, to 851,000. In 1982, it rose another 12 percent. Only perhaps 10 to 25 percent of the cases are believed to be reported.[20]

Early in 1984, the nation was shaken by news of widespread sexual abuse of children in day-care centers. In California, seven adults were charged with 207 counts of sexual abuse at a prestigious Manhattan Beach day-care center. In Chicago, parents filed suit against a center where a janitor was accused of molesting three young girls. In Florida, a Miami man wanted on suspicion of abusing children at his baby-sitting service turned himself in to police. In New York City, Bronx district attorney Mario Merola accused the city's Human Resources Administration (HRA), which oversees 385 city-founded day-care centers, of hampering his investigation of the PRACA day-care center at which three workers had been arrested on charges of sexually abusing children. Top HRA officials resigned in the ensuing scandal. In Florida, a child who stayed at a day-care center contracted gonorrhea of the throat. "How many shocks in a row can the parents take? It's getting unbearable," said a father of a two-year-old who was often in the care of those arrested for abuse in Miami.[21]

The decline of the family, a willingness to violate the law, and society's unwillingness to hold people responsible for their actions have been part of the atmosphere of our society in the recent past. According to William Barret, "The violent dissatisfaction with the prosaic and workable arrangements of society (from the family on up) that permit liberty, is part of the general spiritual sickness of modernity."[22]

A distinguished psychiatrist, Dr. Karl Menninger, suggests that an important reason for the rise of mental illness in the United States is the decline of a sense of individual responsibility and personal worth—a feeling of helplessness and a lack of direction. He argues that people have always learned more from their mistakes than from their success, but when the price of mistakes is eliminated, the challenge, the risk, and the motivation, as well as the sense of direction, are lost.[23]

Father Bruce Ritter, a Franciscan priest and executive director of Covenant House in New York City, has devoted his life to helping homeless and runaway children. Father Ritter has been referred to by President Reagan as one of the "unsung heroes" of our time. In his testimony before a Senate caucus on the family, Ritter stated that,

> the traditional American family is an awesomely strong and resilient institution, but it has probably never been closer to collapse than it is now. For example, from 1970 to 1980, the number of married couples with children under 18 declined, while the number of single-parent households doubled. The divorce rate has tripled since 1960. Of the children who come to Covenant House, less than a quarter have been raised in two-parent homes. In counseling our kids and working with their parents we see day after day the overwhelming emotional and economic burdens that single parenthood imposes — all the more overwhelming because so many single parents assume that role while they are still little better than children themselves.[24]

Father Ritter indicated that 25 percent of the children under the age of fifteen came from situations in which they had been abused in a one-parent, alcoholic family. An alarming number of them, he noted, had been used in commercial sex-for-sale schemes. He lamented that "ours has become a deeply materialistic, even hedonistic culture — a society of consumers."[25]

Can we conclude, then, that these recent trends will simply become more pronounced in the not-too-distant future? Although it is a distinct possibility, given society's propensity for dramatic reversals in values and its penchant for survival, the expansion or even continuance of the past age of license and permissiveness is not likely. Things that seem all-important, modern, and progressive in one era become outdated in another. They are replaced, in many instances, by a

24. Testimony of Father Bruce Ritter, *Congressional Record*, February 1, 1984, p. S714.
25. Ibid.

return to older ideas and values that have been "rediscovered" by a generation unaware of their historical precedents. Already there seems to be a more conservative generation of young people in our high schools and colleges, less interested in challenging authority and denigrating their country and its institutions and more concerned with securing their personal futures.

Robert Nisbet, author of *The History of the Idea of Progress*, says that "there is by now no single influence greater in negative impact . . . than our far-flung and relentless jettisoning of the past." The past, he writes, is vital to the idea of progress:

> It is the future that we are more likely to think of immediately when the idea of progress is brought up. But it was only when men became conscious of a long past, one held in common through ritual and then history and literature, that a consciousness of progressive movement from past to present became possible, a consciousness easily extrapolated to the future. . . . The ancient Greeks, even at the highest point of their exploration of the present, were nevertheless profoundly interested in their past, in finding or recreating its events, in revering it in all that was taught at home, school and temple. . . . The past has loomed large in every age or century of Western history.[26]

That is, the past has loomed large in Western civilization until at least the beginning of our own century.

In *Death of the Past*, J. H. Plumb observes that in all areas of both social and personal life the hold of the past has weakened. Rituals, myths, and the need for personal "roots," which seemed so necessary one hundred or even fifty years ago, are less important. In education and economic activity, the past is regarded as more of an impediment than a guide. Modern family and sexual relations draw no instruction or comfort from the past.[27] It no longer provides authority for the pres-

26. Robert Nisbet, *The History of the Idea of Progress* (New York: Basic Books, 1980), p. 323.
27. Ibid., p. 326.

ent. Indeed, the modern attitude might be that, because it is past, or history, it must be inapplicable to the present.

Prof. Stanley Hoffman of Harvard University sees a growing disconnection with the more distant past. "The past is becoming an object of erudition or diversion, rather than a part of one's own being," and in the educational system, the teaching of history has regressed into social studies and the contemporary.[28] Even in history courses and history texts, Frances Fitzgerald suggests in *America Revisited*, what pupils often find is no past, no history at all, but social studies or current events, "a potpourri of *pasts* each tied to some currently engrossing ideological theme such as ethnicity, sexuality, or an ideological-political framework with disharmony inevitably the result."[29]

Given our apparent disassociation with the past, how can we make projections about the future? Will society continue to move in the same direction we have steered in the recent past, or will we change course? Can we, in fact, really divorce ourselves from our past? Looking at some key areas of social concern today, the family, the aged, and minorities, what might be the future?

The Family

The very nature of the American family is in the process of change. A report prepared by demographers at the Joint Center for Urban Studies of MIT and Harvard and entitled "The Nation's Families, 1960–1990" predicts that by 1990 husband-wife households with only one working spouse will account for only 14 percent of all households, as compared with 43 percent in 1960. Wives will contribute about 40 percent of family income, as compared with about 25 percent now. The report predicts that at least thirteen separate types of household will eclipse the conventional family, including such categories as "female head, widowed, with children" and "male head, previously married, with children." It is predicted that more than one-third of the couples first married in the 1970s will have divorced; more than one-third of the children born in the 1970s

28. Ibid.
29. Ibid., p. 328.

will have spent part of their childhood living with a single parent.[30]

An important element that will affect the future of the family, and that is itself the result of contemporary family structures, is the fertility rate. In the early 1970s, the total fertility rate in the United States reached 2.0 children per child-bearing female, a rate lower even than that during the Great Depression. Fertility trends are an important index of future social development and family formation. Table 2 reviews the data for the past fifty years, corresponding approximately to the modern industrial period. These rates affect population growth, the demographic profile, and family structures in the postindustrial period. In this sense there is no escaping our past.

Table 2 indicates that at the level of fertility for the 1975–1979 period, population actually began to decline by 0.7 percent per year. Although the fertility rate has increased since 1979, the United States has maintained a near zero population growth rate for the past two decades. Since the 1950s, the fertility rate has been cut in half. One commentator notes that

Table 2   U.S. Total Fertility Rate and Intrinsic Rate of Natural Increase

Years	Total Fertility Rate	Intrinsic Rate of Natural Increase per Year (%)
1930–34	2.1	0
1935–39	2.0	−0.2
1940–44	2.5	+0.5
1945–49	3.0	1.2
1950–54	3.3	1.7
1955–59	3.7	2.1
1960–64	3.4	1.9
1965–69	2.6	0.8
1970–74	2.1	0
1975–79	1.8	−0.7

Source: National Center for Health Statistics, in Ben Wattenberg, *The Good News Is the Bad News Is Wrong* (New York: Simon & Schuster, 1984), p. 63.

30. George S. Masnick, *The Nation's Families, 1960–1990* (Boston: Auburn House, 1980), pp. 1–175.

the "baby boom [has] become a Birth Dearth." Americans have gone to "negative replacement."[31]

Declining fertility rates can be attributed to a variety of factors. One obvious explanation is the introduction of contraceptives. The movement of women into the work force is also a factor. Housing costs and tuition have soared, each related to the perceived costs of rearing a child. The rise in abortions is also a significant cause of the declining birth rate. There were 745,000 legal abortions in 1973. By 1980, the number had more than doubled, to 1.55 million. For whites, the number of abortions per 1,000 live births was 175 in 1972. By 1980, it was up to 428. For blacks it went from 223 to 645.[32] The full impact of these figures has not yet hit us. Because of what demographers call the "echo effect" of the baby boom, our population will continue to grow for a time before it begins to experience possibly significant declines.

Although the birth rate is declining for the overall population, the births to older mothers are increasing as women wait longer than ever to begin their families. According to the National Center for Health Statistics, from 1975 to 1978, there was a 37 percent increase in the number of women of age thirty to thirty-four who were having their first child. By 1982, the age group accounted for 6.2 percent of all babies born in the United States. For women aged thirty-five to thirty-nine, the increase was 22 percent. Kathy Weingarten, a clinical psychologist at Wellesley College and the author of a study of mid-life first-time mothers, notes that "it used to be that when a woman decided not to have a baby at age thirty-five, that was it. Now women at age forty-two are still asking themselves the question."[33]

More and more Americans are choosing not to live in families at all, at least for a significant portion of their lives. Between 1970 and 1978, the number of persons aged fourteen to thirty-four who lived alone nearly tripled—rising from 1.5 million to 4.3 million. Today approximately a quarter of all households in the United States consist of a person living alone. At the same time, there is an increase of those the Cen-

31. Ben Wattenberg, *The Good News Is the Bad News Is Wrong* (New York: Simon and Schuster, 1984), p. 63.

32. Ibid.

33. Masnick, *The Nation's Families.*

sus Bureau refers to as "persons of opposite sex sharing living quarters." There were 523,000 unmarried couples living together in 1970, and 1,891,000 by 1983.[34]

The number of female-headed households with one or more children under the age of eighteen more than tripled from 1960 to 1982, from 1.9 million to 5.9 million. As recently as 1970, only 11 percent of American children under eighteen lived with "mother only." By 1982, that percentage had climbed to 20 percent, or more than 12 million children.[35]

Black two-parent families in particular have disintegrated. In 1979, as noted earlier, 55 percent of all black children in the United States were born out of wedlock and into female-headed homes, compared with an estimated 15 percent in 1940. In Washington, D.C., the current figure is 65 percent; in Chicago, 70 percent; and in Harlem, 80 percent of all black children are born out of wedlock. A single woman maintains 41 percent of black families, up from 18 percent in 1940. Twelve percent of white families are headed by single women. An estimated 38 percent of black families are now maintained by two parents.[36]

Sen. Daniel Moynihan (D-N.Y.), reflecting the views of French sociologist Emile Durkheim, laments that we seem to be on the edge of an anarchic society. Moynihan, who, as a member of Lyndon B. Johnson's administration, headed a study group called "The Negro Family: The Case for National Action," concludes that the black family in the urban ghetto is crumbling, which contributes to the continuing cycle of poverty and disadvantage for urban blacks. Moynihan believes that it has become a self-generating phenomenon and is not determined by economic condition.[37]

Births among unmarried black teenagers numbered 133,700 in 1980; one in four black teenaged women were having babies. According to Ann Hulbert, writing in *The New Republic*, black adolescents in the United States have the highest birth rate among teenagers in the developed world, and twice that of white teenaged American girls, who, she says, are themselves "alarmingly fertile." Young mothers and their children

34. Ibid.
35. Wattenberg, *The Good News*, p. 237.
36. Ibid.
37. Ibid.

are a disproportionately large facet of black social and family life.[38]

For many years the black community hesitated to face these facts. Finally, the realization that such trends are growing and are dangerous is increasing. In May, 1984, a Black Family Summit was held at Fisk University and sponsored by the National Urban League and the NAACP. It was attended by scholars and representatives of national black groups. The Urban League called the current situation an "ominous trend." Eleanor Holmes Norton, a law professor at Georgetown University and former chairwoman of the Equal Employment Opportunity Commission, called it a "natural catastrophe in our midst."[39]

Kenneth Clark, a distinguished black psychologist, describes teenaged parenthood in the following way in *Dark Ghetto:*

> In the ghetto, the meaning of the illegitimate child is not ultimate disgrace. There is not the demand for abortion or for surrendering the child that one finds in more privileged communities. In the middle class, the disgrace of illegitimacy is tied to personal and family aspirations. In lower-class families, on the other hand, the girl loses only some of her already limited opportunities by having an illegitimate child; she is not going to make a "better marriage" or improve her economic and social status either way. On the contrary, a child is a symbol of the fact that she is a woman and she may gain from having something of her own. Nor is the boy who fathers an illegitimate child going to lose, for where is he going?[40]

The children of teenaged parents, black or white, are more likely to become teenaged parents themselves. Young fathers, too, are more likely to spring from mothers who had their

---

38. Ann Hulbert, "Vista's Lost Horizons," *New Republic* (August 30, 1982): 18–20; and see "Family Unit Threatened by Rising Illegitimacy," *Washington Times* (September 28, 1982).

39. Dorothy J. Gaitor, "Blacks See Blacks Saving the Family," *New York Times* (May 7, 1984).

40. Ibid.; and see Kenneth Bancroft Clark, *Dark Ghetto: Dilemmas of Social Power* (New York: Harper and Row, 1965), pp. 1–253.

children in adolescence. John Jacob, who gave the opening address at the Fisk University meeting, declared that in concentrating on the wrongs of discrimination and poverty "we may have neglected the fact that there is a lot we can do about our own problems ourselves."[41]

An apparent by-product of the one-parent family and general lack of parental guidance in every context is the decline in academic achievement. A recent survey of the National Association of Elementary School Principals shows that schoolchildren living with only one percent are twice as likely as other students to receive grades in the D and F range and to become high-school drop-outs. Paul Houts, a codirector of the study, explains that one-parent children are more at risk in their personal lives and in their schooling. In addition to having a higher rate of low achievers, one-parent children are consistently more likely to be late for school or subject to disciplinary action. In high school, three times as many single-parent students are expelled and twice as many drop out of school as do children from two-parent families.[42]

These conclusions were supported in a study funded by the Department of Education and released in June, 1983. The study found that single-parent children tended to perform less well academically, and children whose parents were absent because of work or other reasons seemed to score lower on achievement tests. In white, two-parent homes, high-school students whose mothers worked full-time during the school year scored up to nine percentile points lower on tests than students whose mothers never worked. The magnitude of the effect was directly related to how much time the mother worked. Students whose mothers worked only part-time did better than did students whose mothers worked full-time.[43] The Department of Labor reports that almost one-half of the nation's children under six have working mothers and an estimated 1.2 million children are enrolled in day-care centers.

Child-care has traditionally been central to the role of family. Society has not yet adequately assumed the role of paren-

41. Ibid.; see also "A Threat to the Future," *Time* (May 14, 1984), p. 20.
42. Allan C. Brownfeld, "The Element of Parental Responsibility in Education's Decline," *New York Tribune* (August 13, 1983).
43. Ibid.

tal guardian, assuming it is capable of doing so, even though the family unit seems to be dissolving and is incapable of sustaining the traditional role. This is in itself one inescapable reason for the decline of the fertility rate. Family and fertility have been traditional coefficients. Family incentives have weakened as individual interests and opportunities outside of the home have become stronger. Without external social controls and support, the family tends to fall apart, according to Kingsley Davis, a senior researcher at the Hoover Institution. "The special approval of marriage as a sexual and reproductive relationship has been diluted by widespread acceptance of cohabitation, illegitimacy and homosexuality. The stability of marriage has been undermined by easier divorce, culminating in no-fault divorce." And the traditional concept of complementary sex roles has been upset by women's entry into the labor force.[44]

Among the causes of these radical changes in the traditional nuclear family are the conditions of life in the modern urban-industrial society. These are conditions that have only arisen for the most part within the last fifty years. People now participate in the economy as individuals rather than as families. Even the role of the family as a welfare service, taking care of the old and the ill, has been replaced by impersonal government agencies. Specialized agencies, including the schools, have taken over the services the family once performed for children, including the preparation of meals.[45] The family is less essential for survival than it was not long ago, but it may nevertheless provide a more satisfying and enriching environment than any present alternatives.

The family is quite likely to survive the postindustrial period. It has, after all, survived throughout most of human existence in much the same form. It will, however, probably have a more diverse character than the traditional nuclear family—which itself will remain the dominant family structure. A study entitled "The American Family in the Year 2000," completed under the auspices of the American Council of Life Insurance, concludes that there will be more divorces, more single-parent families, and more mixed families from remar-

44. Ibid.
45. Ibid.

riages, but the ideal of marrying and having children will remain a central aspect of American social values.[46]

Fewer Americans than at present will be spending their lives in the framework of the nuclear family over the next fifty years. Families will be of three kinds: families of first marriages, single-parent families, and families of remarriages. The life course of many if not most children will also be different. A child born in the 1980s or after, for example, might well expect to live with both parents for a while, then to live with the mother after a divorce, then with the mother and a stepfather, then alone in his or her twenties, then with someone of the opposite sex without marrying, then marry, get divorced, live alone, get remarried, and end up living alone following the death of the spouse.[47]

Sociologists Andrew Cherlin at Johns Hopkins University and Frank F. Furstenberg, Jr., of the University of Pennsylvania predict that the family will survive, albeit in somewhat different form. It is a very resilient institution and remains much stronger than its critics realize. Although many young adults are living together outside of marriage, there is evidence that cohabitation is not proving to be a lifelong alternative to marriage; it appears to be a new stage in the process of courtship and marriage, or a transition period between marriages. The alternative life-styles popularized in the 1960s, such as communes and "lifelong singlehood," no longer hold much attraction.[48] The sexual revolution of the sixties and seventies may be over. *Cosmopolitan* magazine, in fact, suggests that a sexual counterrevolution may already be under way in America.[49]

Although it is still too early to argue convincingly that a countertrend is under way, the statistics indicate that divorces are declining and marriages are up. A record 2.5 million couples were married in 1982, and for the first time in twenty years the number of divorces was down slightly. Radicals and feminists who scorned marriage in past decades are now less evident. On the contrary, marriage is "in" with ambitious, professional women. Polls taken since 1978 indicate that greater

46. Andrew Cherlin and Frank F. Furstenberg, Jr., "The American Family in the Year 2000," *The Futurist* (June, 1983): 7.
47. Ibid.
48. Ibid.
49. "The Revolution Is Over," *Time* (April 9, 1984): 74.

approval of traditional family ties and reduced support for sexual freedom are developing.[50]

A more conservative or traditional attitude toward sex is also becoming apparent. Polls conducted by *Psychology Today* in 1969 and again in 1983 showed a definite move away from the earlier view held by youths under the age of twenty-two that sex without marriage was okay. Among selected "Who's Who" groups of high-school students, one-fourth had sexual experiences before graduation as compared with 40 percent in 1971. Polls taken at the college level indicated a similar drift away from premarital sex.[51]

It seems clear that family relationships will continue to play a vital role in future society. Divorce, although becoming more rather than less common, is regarded by some as part of the "shopping" process for a permanent mate and does not reflect real disillusionment with marriage as an institution. More people can be expected to delay marriage and, once married, to delay childbearing. And families will remain small, with one or two children the norm. Although the family of the future will be different, it will be easily recognizable. Those who have predicted its demise are wrong. Indeed, the most profound social change of the future will have less to do with the family structure than with the age of the family members.

Aging

American society is aging and will continue to age in the foreseeable future. By 1990, the number of older citizens will exceed thirty-one million, and the teenaged population will shrink to twenty-three million. We are older than we have ever been and we are getting older, says demographer Gregory Spencer of the Bureau of the Census.[52]

Adult life expectancy has increased dramatically in the recent past and promises to improve further. Between 1850 and

50. Ibid.
51. Ibid.
52. "Researchers See Hope for the Family," *New York Times* (October 27, 1984); "10 Forces Reshaping America, a Maturing Society," *U.S. News and World Report* (March 19, 1984): 40–41.

1950, life expectancy increased from thirty-nine to sixty-nine years. Although earlier increases had to do more with lower infant and child mortality, more recently, adult life expectancy, that is, for those over forty, has increased significantly. Declining mortality rates are now attributable to greater longevity for older Americans.[53]

Prof. Eileen Crimmins, a gerontologist at the University of Southern California, has said that a person aged sixty-five can now expect to live to age eighty-one. She predicts that an American aged sixty-five in the year 2000 can expect to live to age eighty-seven. French demographer Jean Bourgeois-Pichat believes longevity will be even greater. A typical sixty-five-year-old living in a Western country in the year 2000 should expect to live to almost one hundred, he says.[54]

The declining birth rate together with the increase in life expectancy is producing an aging society. The baby-boom generation, born between 1946 and 1964, is now moving into middle age. By 1990, the number of people between the ages of thirty and forty-four is expected to increase by 20 percent and to total about sixty million.[55]

The aging of the population is altering society in many ways. It is, for example, producing a decline in the crime rate. Studies show that young people are likely to commit crimes, especially crimes of violence. As their numbers decline, so does crime. Priorities also change for an aging population. Robert Binstock, director of the Policy Center on Aging at Brandeis University says, "We may see schools become less important and long-term health care more important as America becomes a society with fewer smaller children and more older people."[56]

Although older people in general are healthier than ever before, this fast-growing segment of the population, those over eighty-five, includes many who suffer chronic illnesses. This group is expected to number more than 3.5 million by 1990, a jump of almost 1 million over the present level. The surge is almost certain to drive up the costs of Medicare and to in-

53. Ibid.
54. Ibid.
55. Ibid.
56. Ibid.

crease the general costs of private medical care. Longer-lived people enter a threshold where health conditions become more chronic and more expensive, and the quality of life more tenuous.[57]

A report issued by the U.S. Census Bureau in October, 1984, stated that the number of Americans aged sixty-five and over has doubled in the last three decades and could swell to one-fifth of the nation's population in the next fifty years. Continuous, substantial increases are expected to bring the total of elderly Americans to thirty-five million by the turn of the century and to sixty-four million, that is, one in five over the age of sixty-five, by the year 2030. Another report, issued by the Population Reference Bureau in September, 1984, suggests that further improvement in fighting diseases such as cancer and heart disease will provide a longer lifespan for large numbers of the population and will have an unhealthy, long-term impact on the federal budget. Although many will survive into very old age, health and vigor will not necessarily be a part of the picture.[58]

Planning for this kind of future is required now if we are, in fact, to be the managers of change, rather than the victims of that change. Growing longevity will increase government costs and require more taxes. Planning can reduce the magnitude of tax increases and improve the cost and efficiency of medical services. One economist, Barbara Boyle Torry, who participated in a study entitled "Death and Taxes: The Public Policy Impact of Living Longer," says that the question is not whether we can afford to care for the very aged in society, but rather, how to make their lives more useful and vigorous. We must plan efficiently for an aging population.[59]

One important product of the aging population and the declining birth rate will be unparalleled opportunities for young people entering the job market. They will face less competition. And employers will increasingly turn to older, part-time

57. Ibid.

58. Reginald Stuart, "'Old Old' Grow in Numbers and Impact," *New York Times* (June 20, 1983); "First Portraits of the Very Old: Not So Frail," *New York Times* (January 3, 1985).

59. Cristine Russell, "Private Report Shows High Price of Living Longer," *Washington Post* (September 5, 1984).

employees, thus enhancing opportunities for older Americans as well.[60]

Sociologist Aaron Lipman of the University of Miami, who specializes in the study of aging, states that

> aging is a new social problem. In the past, the problem was that people weren't living long enough. Now we have what you might call "mass longevity"—never before have there been so many who are 65 and over. People say George Washington would be surprised if he came back and could see cars, television, and jet planes. But what would really surprise him is how many old people there are now. People from other countries come here and are surprised. "Are most Americans old?" they ask. In less developed countries, the population is younger. Retirement as we know it is fairly new. In the past people worked until they were old and infirm, and then died. Now, many retire at 62. And 62 itself is "younger" in terms of health, literacy, education and skills. It may seem a long time to retirement, but when it comes, it can last for 15 to 20 years. People are living longer, so that when they retire they have more time left.[61]

The idea of retirement is itself beginning to undergo review. Coy G. Eklund, retired chairman of the Equitable Life Assurance Society, argues that retirement should not be universal in its format. People are different and not all want to be "put out to pasture." No one wants to feel ignored or useless. Employees and society must learn to evaluate individuals at any age. If they can make a contribution, they should be gainfully employed, if that is what they choose.[62] Similarly, Alan Pifer, president emeritus of the Carnegie Corporation and head of its aging-society project, says that "age 65 is obsolete." As a result of improved health and increases in longevity, age sixty-five is no longer a realistic dividing line between being middle-aged and elderly. "A great majority of Americans don't age significantly until they are well into their seventies." For the most

60. Ibid.
61. Jack McClintock, "The Greening of America: How Old Is Old?" *New York Tribune* (April 28, 1984).
62. Ibid.

part, they remain vigorous and sound of mind and body. Our view of "old" is based on conditions prevalent in earlier times, when people over sixty-five really were old.[63]

Pifer believes that public and private business policies for older Americans need to be rethought and tuned to the realities of the times. He says that for the third quarter of life, that is, in the fifty-to-seventy-five-year age bracket, there must be the social expectation that a useful and productive life continues. There are, he noted, now over fifty million Americans in this age group, and in another three decades there will be eighty-five million, nearly one-third of the total population. The capacity, and even the necessity, for these people to remain productive will be enormous and must not be ignored.[64]

Mary K. Kouri, a career development counselor and gerontologist with Human Growth and Development Associates of Denver, agrees that the whole idea of retirement must be reviewed. Retirement was supposed to have been a respite and a reward for many years of labor, but for many it has become a burden, both financially and in terms of satisfaction and fulfillment. When Social Security began in 1935, 150 workers paid in to the program for each beneficiary. In 1980 only 3 workers were paying in for each beneficiary, and the system was encountering fiscal shortfalls. The reality, she suggests, is that American society simply cannot afford the marginal economic involvement of a growing proportion of its members —that is, those "older Americans."[65] Economic realities, in other words, may take care of the problem of noninvolvement by the "third-quarter" Americans.

With more Americans aging and fewer coming into the market-place to replace them, there will be little choice but to allow large numbers of people over sixty-five to continue working. Carolyn Byrd supports this view in *The Good Years: Your Life in the Twenty-first Century.* People not only will need to continue to work after the age of sixty-five, but these people will provide an invaluable pool of understanding and

63. Alan Pifer, "Put Out to Pasture, Our Idea of Age 65," *New York Times* (February 7, 1984).
64. Ibid.
65. Ibid.

human experience that machines and younger people simply cannot supply.[66]

Even as we approach and solve the "problem" of aging, the entire concept and even the reality of aging may change significantly in the twenty-first century. We stand on the brink of discovering the very secret of the aging process, many believe, and we may begin to control it within the lifetimes of people living today. In ancient Greece, the average life expectancy was approximately twenty-two years; in colonial America it was approximately thirty-five. Today, some gerontologists believe, significant progress is being made toward the control of aging. It is believed that there is an identifiable genetic "clock of aging" within us that dictates that we will age and die, and it establishes the rate at which this will occur. They argue that we have a good chance of discovering the location (there may be more than one) of the clocks of aging, as well as the nature of their mechanisms and how to interfere with them to our own advantage.

Robert Rosenfeld, author of the widely discussed *Prolongevity* and *The Second Genesis: The Coming Control of Life,* says that for the first time in our history it has become a real possibility rather than a fantasy that we can do something about old age, even eliminate it. Although it is a bizarre idea, the real breakthrough is simply that gerontologists have come to believe that aging is a part of the genetic programming that is built into life when it begins. Just as the fertilized egg is programmed to make each individual an embryo, a fetus, an infant, a child, and an adolescent, the program also includes aging and death. If you can discover what the program is and how it works, you can probably manipulate it to your own advantage, Rosenfeld concludes.[67]

Growing old in America, then, is very likely to be a different experience in the postindustrial economic cycle than it has been in the modern industrial age. It should be a more rewarding, more fulfilling, and, without reservation, a longer experience than ever before.

66. Ibid.
67. Albert Rosenfeld, "Prolongevity: The Extension of the Human Life Span," *The Futurist* (February, 1977): 13.

Minorities

When one thinks of minorities in America today, one ordinarily considers Afro-Americans, Hispanics, and Asians. The accepted view is that these groups suffer from economic and political disenfranchisement and from social exclusion. American minorities have generally stood at the "mudsill" of society. Black Americans argue that conditions for blacks in America are bad and are getting worse. Many minority spokespersons, perhaps necessarily, deny that there has been advancement for their people. In too many cases, they are correct. But the data offer strong evidence of real advancement and achievement, particularly for blacks. What can minorities, such as the Afro-Americans, anticipate in the postindustrial era?

In a report entitled "America's Black Population, 1970–1982," the Bureau of the Census indicated that black-owned businesses increased in value from $473 million in 1973 to $2.2 billion a decade later. Blacks in the civilian work force increased by 31 percent, to 2.7 million, and the average income for black families increased by 6.9 percent, to $19,620. In addition, the number of blacks moving from the inner city to the suburbs has steadily increased. In 1950, there were 1.7 million blacks in the suburbs. The number rose to 2.5 million in 1960, 3.6 million in 1970, and almost doubled by 1980, to 6.2 million. Whereas black suburban residency has increased by 70 percent in that last ten-year period, white residency has risen by 28 percent. In 1984, 23 percent of the black population lived in suburbs, reflecting a sharp rise in both affluence and assimilation.[68]

Black home ownership has also risen considerably since 1940, to the point that almost 50 percent of black families are homeowners, compared with 25 percent earlier. The number of blacks enrolled in colleges and universities has also increased sharply, from about 114,000 in 1950, to 1.2 million in 1982. In the period between 1970 and 1981, white enrollment in colleges rose 37 percent and black enrollment increased by 117 percent.[69] The number of professionals, such as accoun-

68. Wattenberg, *The Good News,* pp. 219–27.
69. Ibid.

tants, computer specialists, school administrators, and engineers, who are black has risen markedly, even since 1970.[70]

Two University of Michigan economists, Glenn Loury and Jerome Culp, believe that minority workers entering the labor market have almost achieved equality with their nonminority counterparts in both skills and earnings. In many instances, they note, black professionals are better rewarded than their white counterparts. They anticipate a reversal of the historical patterns of racial economic inequality in the future.[71] An important element in long-term trends is the improved educational status of the young black.

Blacks have made tremendous strides in improving their educational profile compared to whites. According to the Census Bureau, the median years of school completed by white and black students in the twenty-five to twenty-nine age group are finally comparable (see table 3).

Table 3   Median Years of School Completed, by Race

| | No. of Years Completed | |
Year	Whites	Blacks
1950	12.0	8.6
1960	12.3	9.9
1970	12.6	12.2
1981	12.8	12.6
1982	12.9	12.7

Source: Wattenberg, *The Good News*, pp. 219–27.

Other indexes of black achievement and advancement include the growing number of black military officers. The number of black members of Congress doubled from 10 to 21 between 1970 and 1983. The number of black mayors rose from 48 in 1970, to 251 in 1983, with some of these being mayors of the nation's largest cities, including Detroit, Los Angeles, Chicago, Philadelphia, Washington, D.C., Atlanta, and New Orleans. The number of black state legislators rose from 169 to

70. Ibid.
71. Ibid.

379.[72] Despite these gains, blacks still tend to make up the greater number of those Americans living at the poverty level and those convicted of crimes. Unemployment seems to affect minorities first, and particularly young blacks.

Black families actually experienced a decrease in real earnings in the period 1970–1980, in contrast to white families. Ben Wattenberg, of the American Enterprise Institute, attributes the decline to several factors, but most prominently to the fact that, whereas in white families the wife entered the job market and increased the family income, in the black family the woman was usually already employed. In fact, as the black family disintegrated, the role of family bread winner increasingly devolved upon the female head of family. Instead of obtaining two wage earners, as white families often did, black families have more often lost one. The changes, Wattenberg explains, are really demographic changes rather than income changes.[73] Median black income actually rose from $13,325 to $14,830 in the same time period and rose as a function of white income from 58 percent to 66 percent.[74]

Not only the statistics have improved for black Americans, but the attitudes and the social environment have distinctly improved since the days of sit-ins, boycotts, riots, and blockades. A recent Harris poll concluded that about 70 percent of Americans hold essentially nonracist views.

Asians and Hispanics have been among the fastest-growing minorities in the United States over the past half century. Immigration from Asia and Latin America has risen sharply, in part under the special circumstances generated by the Cuban revolution and the wars in Korea and Vietnam. Asians and Hispanics have entered the lists as among the most active business entrepreneurs.

In New York City, fruit-and-vegetable markets run by Koreans are popping up. The Murray Hill section along lower Lexington Avenue, once an Armenian neighborhood, now is called Little India, an area where women in saris browse through stores that sell curry and chutney. Immigrants have

72. Ibid.
73. Ibid.
74. Gordon Green and Edward Welnick, "Changing Family Composition and Income Differences," (Washington, D.C.: U.S. Bureau of the Census, August, 1982).

changed the face of the Flushing district of Queens. At least ten thousand Chinese, Koreans, Indians, Filipinos, and Japanese live in a Flushing neighborhood with a total population of seventy-six thousand. These newcomers have caused little friction with the predominantly Irish and Jewish residents of the area. T. J. Lusardo, chairman of the Greenpoint Savings Bank, believes the Asians are hard-working, thrifty, and a stabilizing influence.[75]

Asian-American youth, from families that constitute about 1.5 percent of the total U.S. population, made up twelve of the forty finalists in the Westinghouse Science Talent Search in 1983. In that year 10 percent of Harvard's freshman class was Asian-American. Although no more than 15 percent of California high-school graduates qualify for admission to the University of California system, about 40 percent of the Asian-Americans do. The Asian-American immigrant is reminiscent of the East European immigrant who came in the 1950s, says Bronx High School of Science principal Milton Kopelman. They want to work, and they have great respect for education. According to William Liu, who directs the Asian-American mental health center at the University of Illinois Chicago campus, the Confucian ethic predisposes the Asian student to scholastic achievement as a way of repaying the infinite debt to parents and of showing filial piety.[76] Principal Norman Silber of Chicago's Lane Technical High School says that Asian kids have terrific motivation. "They feel it is a disgrace to themselves and their families if they don't succeed."[77]

Asians were the fastest-growing ethnic group in the United States during the 1970s. Some population researchers expect the nation's Asian population to grow at an even faster rate during the 1980s because of an above-average birth rate in many Asian communities and accelerated legal and illegal immigration. Recent migrations have produced enterpreneurs such as Dr. An Wang, the founder of Wang Laboratories, a pioneer in word processing, and Hiroaki Aokie, who created the Benihana of Tokyo restaurant chain. Migration has produced executives like Ming Hsu, who came to the United States from

75. Robert Lindsey, "The New Asian Immigrant," *New York Times* (May 9, 1982).
76. Ibid.
77. Ibid.

China in the closing days of World War II and who became a vice-president of RCA Corporation.[78]

In an article titled "The New Asian Immigrants," Robert Lindsey describes the immigrant communities that are taking root in the United States, from Boston to Seattle. Immigrants, he notes, are reviving old, deteriorating neighborhoods like parts of the Lower East Side in New York and fringes of the North Beach section of San Francisco. A stretch of Olympic Boulevard in Los Angeles has become the thriving center of a Korean community of some one hundred thousand, and Clark Street on the North Side of Chicago has become an attractive Oriental enclave. Houston has four Asian-language newspapers. There are large concentrations of Japanese and other Asian business leaders in the offices of many American and Asian or European companies doing business in America.[79]

George Gilder, in *The Spirit of Enterprise*, explains that immigrants have historically brought entrepreneurial skills and new enterprise into the United States. Modern immigrants do no less. Gilder argues that "no group has played it out with the energy and resourcefulness of the Cubans who fled Castro's Cuba in rage and fear and settled first in Miami, Florida."[80] When the Cubans arrived in the early 1960s, the city was in a depressed economic condition. Over one thousand homes under Federal Housing Administration mortgages had been abandoned in the inner-city area. Many local residents and some experts predicted nothing but chaos, cost, and ethnic friction.[81] The final result was markedly different.

The Cuban immigrants seem to have contributed significantly to economic rejuvenation. "In a once ghostly three and half square miles, Little Havana boasts what the Latin Chamber of Commerce catalogues" as over ten thousand Cuban-owned business establishments ranging from restaurants, supermarkets, banks and travel agencies, to photo studios, bookstores, bakeries, and funeral parlors. Indeed, Cuban business activity has spilled all over Dade County. The

---

78. Ibid.
79. Ibid.
80. George Gilder, *The Spirit of Enterprise* (New York: Simon and Schuster, 1984), pp. 93–111.
81. Ibid.

immigrants, says Gilder, have been anything but a problem for Miami. They revived the stagnant inner city and "transformed the entire Miami economy, making it into a new gateway to Latin American commerce, a new financial access between Europe, the United States, and the 30 nations and 342 million people to the south."[82]

Most recently, 125,000 Mariel "boat people" have arrived from Cuba, and some 45,000 Haitians, most of whom have made their homes in Florida. By 1984, 95 percent of the Mariel boat people from Cuba had found or created work. For the modern immigrant to the United States, Florida, California, and Texas have proved most receptive in terms of job opportunities and have been the leading havens for immigrants. Gilder calls the post-Castro immigration from Cuba the most successful large immigration in the history of a nation of immigrants. The triumph of socialism and tyranny abroad, Gilder says, speaking of those refugees from the Russian czars, the German kaisers and Adolf Hitler, and the communist revolutionaries, has historically resulted in the enrichment of America.[83]

There is every reason to believe that a new period of entrepreneurial growth and innovation is now beginning, in part due to the leavening of the immigrant, and in part to the new opportunities being created by the high-tech, information, and service industries of the postindustrial cycle. In a free economy, hard work and creativity are still rewarded. Those immigrants who learned firsthand what government manipulation and the deprivation of freedom mean may be teaching us all a vital lesson and reaffirming a basic American value. The American ideal, Thomas Wolfe once said, has to do with the belief that everyone should be able to go as far as his own initiative and ability can take him. It is this ideal that has attracted so many to our shores for so long.

In conclusion, American society is in the process of becoming a much different society. It is likely that the crime index, including violent crimes and burglary, will continue at relatively high but declining levels. The traditional nuclear family is giving way to families of new dimensions, with

82. Ibid.
83. Ibid.

single-parent families in particular on the increase and likely to remain a prominent part of society. Under these circumstances, growing up young in America will not be easy. The traditional life course of the individual will change considerably, such that a child will more likely live in the context of several family structures, including both parents, single-parent, and parent/step-parent. The child will also live longer. The ideal of the traditional family, children, and marriage will remain strong and is already on the rebound. Perhaps the most significant changes in American society over the next fifty years will be those engendered by the aging of Americans.

Demography, in fact, will play a vital role in the social and economic development of society. Simply put, there will be far more older Americans and far fewer younger Americans. Retirement patterns will change as more older Americans remain in the work force. Opportunities for the young and for minorities will be greater than before. Despite the changes, however, the family and American society as we know it will be recognizable in the family and society of the future. In the long term the structures of family and society are characterized by continuity rather than discontinuity.

CHAPTER THREE

A Religious Awakening?

When Alexis de Tocqueville visited the newly organized United States of America and returned to write *Democracy in America,* he was struck by many American Peculiarities, but none so much as the preoccupation with things religious. "In the United States the sovereign authority is religious," he said. He became increasingly conscious of the political consequences of this concern about religion. One has only to reflect on contemporary debates about prayer, the teaching of science and evolution, women in the ministry, adultery, homosexuality, cults, and birth control to be aware of the special mix of religion and politics in modern society. Court decisions and legislation to keep religion out of politics are in themselves political decisions affecting religion.

On the one hand, we hear of a great religious reawakening, reminiscent of the Great Awakening of the eighteenth century or the evangelical movements of the nineteenth. On the other hand, there is evidence of a new religious radicalism or even anarchy indicated by the growing schisms in organized churches and the rise of cults such as the Hare Krishna movement and the Bhagwan Rajneesh following. And we see more young people joining the older, established church groups than ever before. What does it all mean? Only one thing is certain: there is little agreement on what it means. That, however, should not discourage one from thinking about religion in America and where it might be heading, because there is agreement that wherever religious movements go and whatever forms of expression religion takes, Americans are more affected than are people in most of the other affluent Western societies.

To help us assess where we might be going, it is useful to attempt to assess where we are right now. Perhaps there is no better handle on things than that provided by the Gallup polls. One poll conducted by George Gallup attempted to compare the state of religion in America with that in other industrialized nations. When asked two questions, "Do you believe in God?" and "Do you believe in heaven?" the Gallup samples showed extremely high positive responses from Americans: 95 percent said they believed in God; 84 percent said they believed in heaven. Italians showed an 84 percent positive response to a belief in God, and 41 percent to heaven; Great Britain was 76 and 57 percent, respectively; West Germany, 72 and 31 percent; France, 62 and 27 percent; and the Japanese response showed 39 percent believing in God, and 20 percent in heaven.[1]

Gallup surveys of Americans who had attended church "within the last seven days" taken in 1969 and 1983 showed little change in the percentiles. But Gallup pointed out that this suggests a real increase in religious observance inasmuch as people under thirty are usually less active in churches than their elders. Thus, as American society became younger, a larger proportion of the young than usual elected to attend a church. This analysis would also suggest that as America ages, the nation's churches might anticipate a disproportionally large increase in membership. There already may be evidence of this trend. Considerably more Americans in 1980 thought religion was increasing its influence over American life than was true in 1970.[2]

The state of religion in modern America is a measurement not only of growing numbers of churchgoers and members, but of the growth in ecclesiastical choices. The United States has always had an "astonishing religious variety" when compared to Europe, or even its closest neighbors, Canada and Mexico. It has something of a "free market" in religion. Whereas

---

1. Ben Wattenberg, *The Good News Is the Bad News Is Wrong* (New York: Simon and Schuster, 1984), p. 276.
2. *Public Opinion Magazine* (March, 1979): 9.

86 percent of church members in Canada belong to three denominations, Roman Catholic, the United Church of Canada, and the Anglican Church of Canada, nineteen different groups must be aggregated before 86 percent of American membership is tabulated.[3]

The 72.4 million Protestants in the United States belong to 186 denominations and worship at 300,000 churches. The country's 5.8 million Orthodox, Conservative, and Reform Jews have 5,000 synagogues; its Eastern churches have 3.8 million members divided into 17 different religious bodies with 1,500 churches. The 50 million Catholics in America have 25,000 churches. Each year thousands of young people leave home and follow one of the charismatic cult leaders, gurus, or self-styled messiahs. The 1,500 religious cults in the United States enroll some 3 million members. Americans can worship in a great number of major denominations, or with an astounding number of smaller, independent religious groups.[4] Americans, in other words, have a distinctly different religious environment from that of people anywhere else in the world. Moreover, most Americans are not even aware that they are different in this way.

An assessment of religious developments in America by the London *Economist* concluded that as of 1984 the United States was deeply and uniquely (for a wealthy Western nation) religious. Not only did more Americans go to church than did Europeans, but those who did not attend still professed to strong belief.[5] Foreign observers and American theologians are aware of the apparent religious revival going on in the United States among men and women of all faiths, and particularly among the young. Joseph Fichter, a Jesuit who teaches sociology at Loyola University in New Orleans, says, "God is popular again. Everyone is talking about Jesus." There has been, he said, "an awakening of dormant Christians," which contradicts the much-touted spread of secularism, materialism, and scientism in American society.[6] Protestant theologian Rich-

3. Edmund Fawcett and Tony Thomas, *The American Condition* (New York: Harper and Row, 1982), p. 407.

4. Ibid.

5. "The Year Things Change," *The Economist* (December 22, 1984): 51.

6. *The Christian Century* (March 18, 1981): 296.

ard Lovelace believes that the United States is on the threshold of a "major religious awakening."[7]

One striking aspect of contemporary religious developments is the decline of the mainline Protestant denominations—the Episcopalians, the Presbyterians, the Methodists, and the United Church of Christ—and the rise of the fundamentalist and evangelical groups. Burton Yale Pines believes that you really cannot quantify what is going on in the American religious scene. It is not a matter of church membership, but of the nature of faith itself. Americans of all age groups and social backgrounds are catering to the churches and the televised religious programs, which offer the "old-time religion," with a heady dose of scripture, an inspiring liturgy, an explicit statement of values, and a "stern code of morals that makes a clear distinction between right and wrong." The new religious ferment concentrates on ministering to the spiritual needs of the people rather than launching crusades to reform social, economic, or political institutions.[8]

Americans, Pines says, are rediscovering traditional religion after a long period of experimentation, liberalism, and permissiveness. This new movement has many faces, including born-again Christians, fundamentalists, evangelicals, charismatics, and increasingly observant Jews.[9] Wade Roof, a sociologist at the University of Massachusetts, notes that there has been a great change in the way the world looks at the religious fundamentalist, who not so long ago seemed to be out of step with the modern world and science, but who now seems to be "walking with confidence."[10] But there has also been a peculiar American flavor to this new conservatism.

Discussing the reason why "the more conservative social mood of the past few years, supported by the growth of church-based pressure groups such as the Moral Majority, has done little to change the way many Americans conduct their private lives," the London *Economist* concluded that most Americans are like their president (who is divorced and an indifferent churchgoer); that is, they are "stern in theory but tol-

7. Ibid.
8. Burton Yale Pines, *Back to Basics* (New York: William Morrow and Co., 1982), p. 185.
9. Ibid.
10. *New York Times* (November 11, 1979).

erant in practice." Even fundamentalist groups have an amazing breadth of tolerance. Almost no Americans, for example, advocate using state power to enforce social or religious beliefs. Most are very jealous of the guarantees of individual rights as opposed to the intervention or manipulation of the state.[11] It may also be that the very diversity of American faiths and congregations requires toleration.

There is no disputing, however, the conservative mood of the American religious scene. Some journalists and theologians suspect that liberal Protestantism is an "endangered species." Until the mid-1960s, almost every major denomination in the United States increased its membership, but since then, despite large population increases, most mainline churches have lost members. United Methodist church membership declined from more than 11 million members, to 9.7 million between 1965 and 1980. The Presbyterian church lost 0.5 million members, the Episcopal church about 600,000 members, the American Lutheran church 200,000, and the Disciples of Christ about 700,000 members.[12]

Conversely, the charismatic or evangelical groups experienced strong membership growth. Southern Baptist membership grew by 2.5 million members; Seventh-Day Adventists added 170,000 members; the Mormon church added almost one million members; the Jehovah's Witnesses added almost 200,000 members; and the Assemblies of God, 350,000 members. Roman Catholic membership also grew, by almost 4 million in the same period.[13] If these shifts in church membership continue, a number of the major Protestant denominations could cease to exist by the year 2050.

Why are the conservative churches growing and the older, mainline Protestant denominations losing members? A Methodist minister, Dean Kelley, believes that what is important in religion is not so much the doctrine, but how the church "gathers the lambs unto its bosom and protects and supports and strengthens them and keeps them there." The churches that are lax and permissive are declining, he said, and those that are maintaining clear and rigorous standards are expand-

11. "The Year Things Change," p. 51.
12. *The Christian Century* (January 2, 1980), p. 4.
13. George Gallup, Jr., and David Poling, *The Search for America's Faith* (Nashville: Abingdon Press, 1980), p. 10.

ing. The conservative churches portray confidence and offer authoritative answers to the complex problems of modern life. People are attracted to those groups that profess to know what they are doing and whose members seem to practice what they preach.[14]

George Gallup has concluded from his surveys that Americans are, at least outwardly, very religious. Nine of ten Americans express a religious preference. A vast majority admit that religion is very or fairly important in their lives. Nine of ten Americans believe in God, most of these in a very personal God. Moreover, a majority of Americans profess a belief in both heaven and hell, and about half believe in the Devil, and for many of these the Devil is a very personal Devil. One cannot, he said, exaggerate the importance of the "religious dynamic" in American life. The dynamics of religion often have more to do with what we think and say than do our political affiliation, education, sex, or where we live.[15] Religion has a pervasive, and not necessarily conscious, influence on our lives. One of the modern realities is that religion has always been there; it is simply re-emerging in the consciousness of more and more Americans.

The growing popularity of courses in religion in the nation's schools and colleges provides evidence of the new awareness of religion. Nine hundred institutions of higher learning now offer religious studies or a religion-related curriculum, and some seventeen hundred faculty teach such courses.[16] Whereas religious studies in the 1960s attracted many students to courses in mystical Eastern religions and radical theologies, the students currently enrolled in religious studies seem to be more interested in Western religious thought. They are eager to relate current political, social, and technological problems to their faith, and they are concerned with philosophical questions of ethics and personal morality in a theological context.[17]

Modern students of religion are now-oriented. They are much less interested in religious history than in social and

14. Dean Hoge and David Rozen, eds., *Understanding Church Growth and Decline, 1950–1978* (New York: Pilgrim Press, 1979), p. 34.
15. "Interview with George Gallup, Jr.," *New York Times* (November 1, 1984).
16. Curtis J. Sitomer, "Religious Studies Programs Are Popular at U.S. Universities," *Christian Science Monitor* (April 30, 1984).
17. Ibid.

moral problems they consider "relevant." Thus, a popular
course in religion at the University of California, Santa Barbara, is entitled, "Scientific Responsibility, Technological Unemployment, and the Arms Race." The class deals with ethics
and value problems in a technological world. Many of the students are computer and engineering majors. They are like a
lot of people who wake up at 3:00 A.M. wondering what it's
all about. "People are starved for spirituality," philosopher Jacob
Needleman at San Francisco State University says; "it's a need
as basic as anything else."[18]

A *New York Times* writer, Gene I. Maeroff, visited a
classroom at Rutgers University and said it "sounded like Sunday school." The topic of discussion was God and Martin
Luther's belief that sin can be overcome only by faith in Jesus,
and that faith is itself a gift of grace. Just at the time that public schools have become the focus of political debates over
prayer and the separation of church and state, religious studies
are thriving in the institutions of higher learning, including
the publicly supported universities. Enrollments in religious
studies are generally strong. Although few students at the universities major in religion, the elective courses are a popular
way of satisfying requirements in the humanities.[19]

At the University of Virginia the Department of Religion
was not created until 1967, but now is one of the largest fac-
ulties in the United States, with twenty-three full-time members. Three hundred students will fill a lecture hall to listen
to Kyle McCarter discuss the Old Testament, and an equal
number will enroll in Harry Gamble's course on the New Testament. Nathan A. Scott, Jr., is department chairman and oc-
cupant of one of three endowed chairs in religious studies at
the University of Virginia. He attributes the enormous success of the program to "very powerful teachers."[20] Lawrence S.
Cunningham at Florida State University attributes the interest in religious studies in part to natural curiosity. Students
want to know about religion, no matter what their own experience of faith may be. Cunningham's course on religion
and literature examines belief and nonbelief from the van-

18. Ibid.; "Bhagwan's Realm," *Newsweek* (December 3, 1984): 34–38.
19. Gene I. Maeroff, "Religious Studies Are Thriving," *New York Times*
(October 23, 1984).
20. Ibid.

tage points of such novelists as James Joyce, Walker Percy, and Mary Gordon.[21]

The popularity of religious studies on the campus has caught many educators and theologians by surprise. It contradicts the trend toward increased secularization of university life and the intellectual dominance of "naturalism" and science. Prof. Carl F. H. Henry, founding editor of *Christianity Today*, says that if ever a generation might expect to be lost to a supernatural faith such as the Judeo-Christian heritage, it would be the present generation. There are the students who have joined the evangelical Christian movement and whose devotion, faith, and morality are in marked contrast to the permissiveness of the secular college campus.[22]

The professors as well as the students are reassessing the subject of morality and Christian theism. Three recent presidential addresses of the American Philosophical Association (APA) have concerned the subject of Christian theism. The Society of Christian Philosophers has developed within the APA. The Institute of Advanced Christian Studies has begun issuing paperback textbooks that explore Christian perspectives of various liberal arts disciplines for use on the junior college level. Academia, says Professor Henry, must recover the conviction and promulgation of shared values—the supreme shared value in the West being a belief in God. Unless we retrieve the vision of God and good, he says, we will "doom man to mistake himself and his neighbor for passing shadows in the night, transient oddities with no future but the grave."[23]

New manifestations of faith, however, are different from the older forms. We may renew or reaffirm the traditional values, but we may also make that reaffirmation of faith in a nontraditional way. William J. McCready, program director of the National Opinion Research Center at the University of Chicago, believes that Americans are turning away from the dictates of organized religion and are drawing on individual spiritual feelings in an effort to define their faith. For growing numbers of Americans, McCready notes, an individual search for meaning has become the central religious experience, re-

21. Ibid.
22. Carl F. H. Henry, "Religion on Campus Strong Despite Secularism," *New York Tribune* (June 9, 1984).
23. Ibid.

placing unquestioning obedience to religious authority. The move is not from "authority to anarchy but to conscience." It has been for some, he confesses, an "uncomfortable, messy transition."[24]

McCready's research center has examined the American conscience since 1972. The studies suggest a considerable change in attitude toward religion. In recent surveys 60 percent of Americans rejected the idea of "absolute moral guidelines," whereas ten years ago only 40 percent of those surveyed did so. More people seem to think of their religious faith in "mythic, imaginative and reflective" terms rather than as an absolute standard for behavior. Religious images such as those involving God, Jesus, and Mary are strongly identified with those people having no formal religious affiliation. More adherents of organized religious institutions now go beyond the required minimum standards of membership to explore the deeper meaning of faith. People no longer want to be merely members, but to be a part of the church, to understand and to identify with its heritage. Although a superficial examination suggests that there is a decline in religion and that this is not a religious society, the real evidence is that people have a strong religious orientation.[25]

It no longer means, McCready believes, that, because a person does not affiliate with a religious group, the person is not religious. For example, about a third of the fifty-two million Roman Catholics in the United States rarely or never go to church, yet they think of themselves as Catholics. Similarly, the rejection of absolutes in doctrine or morality does not necessarily imply a lack of religious feeling. Americans seem to be unaware of the extent to which their fellow citizens hold religious values, he points out. In a survey asking about the Ten Commandments, 85 percent of the people contacted personally embraced them, but they believed that less than half of the rest of the population did so. In other words, Americans think of themselves as religious, but do not think of American society as being religious. McCready believes there is an "erosion of confidence" because people lack a clear pic-

24. Kenneth A. Briggs, "Religious Feeling Seen Strong in U.S.," *New York Times* (December 9, 1984).
    25. Ibid.

ture of America's religious character. But there is no doubt, he says, that religion is a major factor guiding the lives of individual Americans.[26]

One aspect of the individualization or personalization of religion is the organization of many small prayer groups outside of the auspices of the institutional churches. Kenneth Briggs, religion editor of the *New York Times*, points out that more and more Americans are coming "to the realization that the human predicament requires a spiritual answer." He reports that from the burgeoning numbers of retreat houses and spiritual centers the message is the same, that the revival of prayer is the "most powerful, least-documented development within modern American religion today."[27]

Prayer, however, is much in evidence in society, if we but stop to think about the leading religious — and political — issues. What are they? Prayer in the public schools, religion and science, and women as religious leaders. Instead of religion being under attack, these issues are evidence of the groundswell of religious thought and activity. The new religious awakening is different from past movements; it is more personal and introspective. For example, prayer is changing from being considered a form or act of worship into a spiritual involvement.

Prayer

De Tocqueville's observation of the political significance of religion in America is perhaps nowhere so well borne out as in the realm of prayer. Prayer in the public schools is more than an issue involving the separation of church and state; it is a symptom of the redirection or refocusing of American religious practice away from the traditional institutional structures to the person. Whereas when one defined religion as a church or denomination, or even as a set of beliefs, it was reasonably clear when the lines of church and state might be transgressed. But when religion becomes a very individual,

26. Ibid.
27. Kenneth A. Briggs, "America's Return to Prayer," *New York Times Magazine* (November 18, 1984): 106.

personal thing that may best be identified by the practice of praying, the lines of demarcation between church and state become confused. And perhaps so does the Supreme Court.

Kenneth Briggs believes that the "born-again" movement of the 1970s has taken new directions. Instead of revivalism and dramatic conversions, the new phase of the movement emphasizes the inward and individual nature of the soul and a deepening personal faith. Whereas the spiritual leader once required or sought a radical commitment to Christ with a "company of believers," the leader now "commends the path of solitary searching."[28] The Protestant evangelical movement and the Catholic charismatic movement have given way to a quieter, more inner awakening. Some converts to or samplers of Buddhism, Hinduism, and other Eastern religions have discarded those and returned to personal prayer, in which they say they have found the real meaning of life.[29]

The number of Americans seeking prayer counseling at the six hundred retreat centers run by various religious groups has increased dramatically in recent years. The Rev. Thomas W. Gedeon, director of Retreats International, the association of Roman Catholic retreat houses, says that these facilities operate at 80 percent of capacity on most weekends, and many are reserved years in advance. The Rev. William J. Connolly, a Roman Catholic staff member of the nondenominational Center of Religious Development, notes that "some people who are heavily engaged in justice issues come here saying, I believe in the work I'm doing, but I can't continue to do it without a deeper basis," or commitment.[30]

There are critics of the current movement toward prayer. Donald G. Bloesch, a professor of theology at the University of Dubuque's Theological Seminary, argues in *The Struggle of Prayer* that much of what passes for authentic prayer is often something quite different. "In popular fold piety," he writes, "prayer is often understood as a form of self-therapy, a technique to attain self-identity of self-fulfillment," but it is also commonly held that the real answer to prayer does not come

28. Ibid.
29. Ibid.
30. Ibid.

from an outside power but from the act itself. Bloesch says that "authentic prayer" is the conversation of a believer with God and entails words and thoughts.[31]

The Reverend Henri Nouwen, a Dutch Roman Catholic priest on the faculty of Harvard Divinity School, believes that prayer should essentially involve "slowing down" and becoming inwardly attentive to the presence of God. He thinks of prayer as listening. Our culture, he says, is terribly afraid to listen. We prefer to remain deaf. The Latin root of *deaf* is the word for "*absurd*," he points out, and what prayer means is moving from deafness or absurdity to obedience. "Let the word descend from your head to your heart so you can begin to know God. In prayer, you become who you are meant to be."[32]

Psychology has become more popular, Sister Ruth McGoldrick of the Genesis Spiritual Life Center in Westfield, Massachusetts, says, because the church has failed to respond to the spiritual needs of people. The Genesis Spiritual Life Center seeks to "bridge the psyche and the spirit." Elizabeth Oleksak, administrator of the center, believes that "within a person there is often a kingdom of light and a kingdom of darkness." The mission of the center is to lead the people to the light.[33] Spiritualism and spiritualists, mystics and psychics, are manifestations of the heightened concern about those things that science somehow seems unable to answer satisfactorily. At the very height of the "age of science" people are turning away from their past reliance on the scientific answer to all things. There are some things that science does not seem to have an answer to, or at least an answer that satisfies.

Religion and Science

The idea that religion and science are incompatible and that religion is no longer required by modern, sophisticated people is in retreat. Sir John Eccles, a Nobel laureate in medicine and physiology and a pioneer in brain research, argues that we can no longer accept the belief that science can deliver the final truth about everything; rather, it offers hypotheses

31. Ibid.
32. Ibid.
33. Ibid.

about the truth, and those hypotheses change rapidly. Newton's law of gravity, for example, was not the final truth about gravity. Scientific "truths" are being constantly remolded, especially now.[34]

Eccles, who is a neurobiologist and the coauthor of a book with Daniel Robinson entitled *The Wonder of Being Human: Our Being and Our Mind,* believes that science has gone too far in "breaking down man's belief in his spiritual greatness." We have been taught by science that we are insignificant animals who have arisen by chance or through adaptation to a changing environment and that we and our planet are insignificant and lost within the greater cosmos. Religion and science are not at odds, Eccles says. Many of the great scientists have been and are religious. Max Planck, a great physicist, was a practicing Catholic. Albert Einstein believed in a God of the cosmos. Werner Heisenberg, a world-famous physicist, held religious views. Eccles says that he is a "practicing Christian." Agnostics such as Sir Karl Popper and Christians such as Eccles "recognize the great wonder of existence. We believe in both a material world and a mental-spiritual world."[35] It has not been easy to cope with both science and spiritual needs, not for the scientists, for religion, or for the individual.

At the present time religion is attempting to deal with a host of complex new problems that are the result of technological progress, particularly in the area of medical ethics and genetic engineering. Yeshiva University in New York City has added a fourth year to its program for rabbinic ordination to better examine the new scientific and technological advances in the light of religious doctrine and instruction. There are new ethical and moral questions to which traditional teachings have no response. Artificial hearts, animal heart transplants, and high-risk surgery and medical treatment have moral and ethical implications. The new curricula attempt to merge biblical principles with science and technology to give direction in addressing contemporary issues. "Torah and science represent two organic forces living together in an organic symbiosis," says Dr. Moses Tendler, a biologist and pro-

34. "A Conversation with Sir John Eccles," *U.S. News and World Report* (December 10, 1984): 80.
35. Ibid.

fessor of Talmud at the seminary. "Neither can survive alone. The clarification of physiological, anatomical and biochemical data must be a part of the rabbi's analytical process. Only then can Jewish law be applied and understood."[36]

A rabbi, says Tendler, cannot respond to a woman's inquiry as to whether she should undertake a sterility-management program by saying, "I don't know. I'm a rabbi, not a doctor." Rabbis must be familiar with medical procedures allowed under religious law. To be sure, the seminaries and the rabbis are not just responding to the intellectual or religious issues raised by science. They are being forced to respond to the needs of a well-informed and sophisticated laity, who are also interested in adhering to the strict traditions of Jewish law.[37]

Protestants, Catholics, and Jews are demanding more of their churches, their leaders, and their seminaries. Religious leaders can no longer cast out science or high-technology because it does not conform to older doctrines or practices. Religion must encompass science, just as science, indeed, must recognize the limitations of the truths it purports to find and recognize the role of faith and spirit in the delineation of the human experience.

In many small ways, religion has seized on high-tech and science to spread spiritual teachings. The radio and television ministry are now being supplemented by the at-home personal computer ministry. The *Wall Street Journal* reports that some families, such as the Kellys of Stockbridge, Georgia, gather around their Apple home computer in the evenings and sing along as the computer plays hymns. The Kellys have started a bimonthly magazine called *Christian Computing*. Computers are being used for everything from writing sermons to playing educational games such as "Bible Baseball."[38]

World, Inc., a subsidiary of American Broadcasting and a major publisher of books and records, has introduced a religious computer game. Zondervan Corporation, of Grand Rapids, Michigan, is experimenting with the sale of religious

36. "Yeshiva Lengthens Rabbinic Studies Program," *New York Times* (December 17, 1984).

37. Ibid.

38. William M. Bulkeley, "Churches, Congregations Increasingly Use Personal Computers to Enhance Worship," *Wall Street Journal* (December 12, 1984).

computer programs in its bookstores. Church management programs for accounting, word processing, mailings, and membership tracking are available. The Christian Computer Users Association reports that about three thousand churches now use computers. Members of the South Congregational Church in Hartford, Connecticut, assembled four Zenith 100 computers from kits several years ago and use them heavily for sermon preparation and mailings. "They are a godsend," according to the pastor.[39] Computer programs are also available for Bible study and religious education.

The King James version of the Bible is available on computer disks. Programs let users search for particular words and will print out applicable passages in which they appear. The programs are similar to concordances, which alphabetically list words from the Bible and tell where to find them. A program called "Scripture Scanner" permits users to compare passages from different parts of the Bible side by side on the screen. A word processing program for ministers allows them to prepare sermons or Bible studies and key in appropriate passages without having to type them out. A Gramcord project developed at Trinity Evangelical Divinity School allows the student to compare grammatical construction of the Greek language New Testament in an effort to better understand the meaning of the phrases. This technique helped resolve a controversy over the phrase "the spirit of God and glory" as a reference to one rather than to two spirits.[40]

For Jewish studies, Davka Corporation of Chicago sells a $250 word processor with Hebrew characters. Davka's president, Irving Rosenbaum, a former president of Hebrew Theological College, says, "We are intent on bringing religion into the world of technology." Davka also sells a game designed to teach the story of Hanukkah, and it offers a game called "Philistine Ploy," which is based on the Book of Judges. In the game, the user plays a lost Israelite eradicating hostile Philistine warriors. It is a game, the company advises, "which took 3,000 years to create."[41]

39. Ibid.
40. Ibid.
41. Ibid.

Women, the Family, and Religion

In recent decades science has interceded strongly in religious practices and doctrine, as well as in family life, by making birth a matter of personal choice. Most sexually active American women use or have access to contraceptives. There are each year about 1.5 million abortions performed in the United States. Every denomination, and particularly the Roman Catholic, has been affected and often challenged by the feminist movement on issues not only relating to birth control, the right to life, divorce, and child care, but on women in the ministry.

The Second Vatican Council set the tone for major changes in Catholic thinking when it seemingly accepted the right of Catholic laypeople to question the authority of the church when it appeared inconsistent with "informed conscience." But in 1968, Pope Paul VI wrote the encyclical *Humanae Vitae*, banning all artificial birth control. Catholic scholars wrote dissents and Catholics generally rebelled and have been rebelling ever since.[42] An estimated one-fourth of the abortions in a given year are sought by Catholic women, and an estimated 90 percent of Catholic women use contraceptive methods not approved by the church, according to a 1982 study by the National Center for Health Statistics. There are also an estimated eight million divorced Catholics, and a majority of those who have remarried have done so outside of the church.[43]

Despite the vigorous efforts of Pope John Paul II to reassert the authority of the church over issues of sexual morality, the evidence is that America's fifty-three million Catholics are inclined to go their own way. It has become difficult to command obedience from the clergy or the laity. American priests and nuns are accepting as their major responsibility the meeting of the everyday spiritual needs of the faithful, and they accept or tolerate their people's independent conscience.[44] As is true in the Protestant and Jewish faiths, the churchgoers

42. Elaine Sciolino, "American Catholics, a Time for Challenge," *New York Times Magazine* (November 4, 1984): 40.
43. Ibid.
44. "Women of the Cloth: How They're Faring," *U.S. News and World Report* (December 3, 1984): 76.

and believers are better informed and better educated and more questioning. Churches of every denomination are required to deal directly with the new independence of conscience and informed individualism.

Women now constitute about 5 percent of all clergy. Their number has risen from about six thousand in 1973 to sixteen thousand by 1984. Seminaries report a continuing rise in female enrollment. In the Episcopal church, which officially sanctioned women priests in 1976 after two years of bitter debate, women now compose about 10 percent of the ten thousand clergy and constitute one-third of the fifteen hundred seminarians. But the controversy over women priests continues in the Episcopal church. Bishops in a number of the dioceses still refuse to ordain women, and few women hold leadership positions.[45] Elsewhere women have done somewhat better.

The United Church of Christ has ordained women since 1853 and actively promotes them to leadership positions. The Rev. Carol Joyce Brun holds the highest position of any churchwoman, having been elected church secretary of the United Church of Christ in 1983. The church also has one of the highest ratios of clergywomen to membership of any main denomination, about 1,000 for each 1.7 million members. Women make up about one-half of the denomination's seminarians. The United Methodist church guarantees a first appointment for all ordained women. The church now has 1,500 women clergy and 2 of the 46 bishops are women; another, Marjorie Suchocki, is dean of Wesley Theological Seminary in Washington, D.C.[46]

The Jewish faith is also opening its door to women. Except for the Orthodox, all the major movements—Reform, Reconstructionist, and Conservative—train women for the rabbinate. "Women have found equality of opportunity," says Rabbi Alfred Gottschalk, president of Hebrew Union College in Cincinnati, who ordained the first woman rabbi in 1972. "The real test is whether women will get prestigious temples in the next few years when our number gets larger," says Rabbi Debra Hachen, who was ordained in 1980 and heads the 160-family

45. Ibid.
46. Ibid.

Congregation B'nai Shalom in Westborough, Massachusetts. Her congregation has dealt with issues associated with clergy-women, including maternity leave and the need for more flexible hours.[47]

The Southern Baptist Convention went on record in the summer of 1984 in opposition to the ordination of women, although more than three hundred women have been ordained and the numbers continue to grow. The resolution has forced Baptists to take a stand on the issue, and women in the ministry are inclined to see that as a positive step, rather than a defeat. Although there are many options open to women in the Roman Catholic church, the priesthood does not seem to be one of them for the foreseeable future.

Although there are obstacles to women in positions of religious leadership, recent strides have been tremendous. The number of women in the seminaries has risen from about 10 percent to 25 percent in the past decade, which suggests to one theologian, Rebecca Chopp of the University of Chicago Divinity School, that by the year 2000, the majority of the clergy could be women.[48]

A less obvious but equally significant aspect of the women's liberation movement has been the growing trend toward interfaith marriages. For example, Jewish leaders are concerned about the number of Jews marrying non-Jews and fear that Judaism may be headed for extinction in the United States. Rabbi Ephraim Buchwald of the Lincoln Square Synagogue in New York City believes that Judaism is in a state of siege. He advises "higher walls, stronger shelters, and more committed Jews in order to reduce the threat of Jewish extinction in America." In this case the threat is not from a hostile environment, but from a benevolent one. The Harvard Center for Population Studies projects that, unless current trends toward intermarriage are altered, there may be only ten thousand identifiable Jews left in America by 2076.[49]

Traditionally, only those children born of a Jewish mother were considered to be Jewish. Reform Judaism, however, has adopted the policy that permits children born of non-Jewish

47. Ibid.
48. Ibid.
49. Natalie Gittleson, "American Jews Rediscover Orthodoxy," *New York Times Magazine* (September 30, 1984): 41, 60–61, 63.

mothers and Jewish fathers to be considered Jews. Reform Judaism also welcomes converts, usually non-Jewish marriage partners. But most Jewish rabbis and leaders lament the trend toward intermarriage. Rabbi Joseph Weinberg of the Washington Hebrew Congregation declared in a sermon that, "what no Pharaoh, Titus, Torquemada or Hitler was able to achieve, we are doing to ourselves. Of all the new dating, mating and procreating patterns of American life . . . none threatens a more lethal blow than that of intermarriage."[50]

Most rabbis still refuse to perform interfaith marriages. But just as have the Catholics, American Jews are making their own free choices, and some rabbis are supportive, or at least tolerant. As Rabbi Stanley Rabinowitz of a Washington, D.C., synagogue has declared, the only way to avoid intermarriage is to live in an isolated ghetto, and he, for one, is not ready to pay that price. "Having entered the mainstream of American life, I'm willing to take the chances. It's a fair trade."[51]

Ironically, there was a time when the Jews had a more tolerant, if not positive, attitude toward intermarriage. The first known instance of a rabbi officiating at an intermarriage ceremony was in Leipzig, Germany, in 1849. Rabbi Samuel Hodheim, a founder of German Reform Judaism, said that intermarriage was an expression of man's noblest spiritual impulses. Such a marriage does nothing less than "affirm that we are all children of one Father who created us all. This represents the true religion, and the young couple its highest exemplars."[52] Similarly, although he is one of few, a Georgia rabbi sees intermarriage as a rare opportunity to enhance and enrich Jewish life.[53]

Thus Americans are charting new paths in religious observances as more and more marriages comprise individuals from different religious traditions. Pat Canes, who is Christian, describes the manner in which she and her Jewish husband celebrate Christmas and Hanukkah with their three children:

50. Virginia Inman, "One in 35 Jews in U.S. Adopted the Religion," *Wall Street Journal* (April 16, 1984); Janet Wallach, "Intermarriage—the Disappearing American Jew," *Washington Post Magazine* (November 11, 1984).

51. Wallach, "Intermarriage."

52. Gary Putka, "As Jewish Population Falls in U.S., Leaders Seek to Reverse Trends," *Wall Street Journal* (April 13, 1984).

53. "Brief," Memorandum from the American Council For Judaism, summer, 1983.

> Christmas lights and menorah candles glow in our home, both providing a warm spark amidst December's chill. Hanukkah and Christmas, two distinct feasts, need not be homogenized to offer hope to a world filled with religious bigotry, misunderstanding and persecution. For our family that hope is deep and personal because my husband is Jewish and I am Christian. To add to the spirit of the season, my spouse was born on Christmas eve in Israel. We turned what could be a serious holiday problem into a joyous celebration.[54]

The Canes's relatives include Christians, Jews, and nonbelievers who all gather for the Christmas season in the Canes home around December 24. They respect each other's beliefs and symbols and do not feel threatened or coerced in the way they accept or deny a belief in God.

Interfaith marriages are but one aspect of the ecumenical religious movement under way in the United States. One of the most difficult of all problems for the established churches and faiths and for the traditional one-faith family to deal with has been the propensity of many young Americans to leave the church and the faith of their parents and to accept a new belief system that seems to have no roots in the old. Every year thousands of young people turn their backs on family, friends, and traditional ways of living to join one or another of the estimated twenty-five hundred communal groups in North America. Their values, dress, and behavior seem totally alien.

The Cults and
American Religious Radicalism

Saul W. Levine, head of the Department of Psychiatry at Sunnybrook Medical Center in Toronto, has studied many of the young people who have joined religious cult groups. He describes his findings in *Radical Departures: Desperate Detours to Growing Up*. Levine believes that "radical departures" create more fear, agony, anger, and disgust among average families than any other situation. Although most people accept

---

54. Ibid.

the idea or explanation that the cults are hostile to the values of the mainline churches and to middle-class standards, there is considerable confusion and disagreement as to what their attraction is and who is being attracted. The prevalent opinion is that the young people who join the cults are troubled kids, academic failures, loners from embattled homes, or drug addicts. Mental health experts tend to see these dropouts as a manifestation of a pathology. The most charitable view is that the young people may have been innocents who got brainwashed. But Levine found the radical converts to be "right off the cover of *The Saturday Evening Post.*"[55]

Levine also believes that the groups he has studied are really not deserving of the "cult" label. They are really not guilty of excesses or alien actions and ideas. Rather, to the families of those who join, they seem radically opposed to the families' own intellectual, spiritual, and social standards. To be sure, the radical groups do have similarities. Most have a fantasized view of the omniscience of their leaders, a rigid belief system that excludes the outside world and a studied strangeness that gives them a unique identity. What makes the groups appear particularly radical is the sudden and total transformation of the convert.[56]

In the case of none of the more than four hundred subjects in fifteen groups that Levine has studied since 1969 was the sudden leave-taking by the young joiners anticipated by the family or friends. Instead, the decision to join one of the communal religious groups was called "out of character" by parents and family members. But Levine has concluded, after examining all of the cases, that the radical departures actually make sense, despite the appearance of irrationality. Young people in this society are faced by well-meaning, but very real obstacles to growing up. A radical departure that embraces a "strangeness that unnerves, the hostility that enrages, and even the euphoria that puzzles" is an expression of belief and belonging that adolescents use as catalysts in growing up. Of those who leave, 90 percent return within two years, Levine discovered, and virtually all of them leave the group with

55. Saul Levine, "Radical Departures: Desperate Detours to Growing Up," excerpts published in *Psychology Today* (August, 1984): 30.
56. Ibid.

which they had identified. Most important, they resume their previous lives and find satisfaction in the middle-class world they had abandoned. In short, he says, they use the "radical departure" to grow up.[57]

Levine also discovered that the belief systems of the various communal groups most often matched the ideals of the joiner's family. A young woman who joined the Children of God, he said, could as easily have joined several such groups whose teaching basically reflected her Sunday school lessons. The convert seeks a new peace, a unity, and a spirituality that have been promised but never found. Belonging, he says, is the heart of a radical departure. The radical groups take comfort in unity—all doing the same thing, eating the same food, dressing the same, speaking the same stock phrases, and working for the same cause. It is easier to be a part of the group self than for the adolescent to continue the struggle to find his or her own independent self.[58]

Although some observers have charged that these new radical groups are holding members against their will and use a variety of forms of compulsion, Levine has reached different conclusions. He points out, for example, that of every five hundred youngsters who are approached, only one actually joins. Relatively few youths are actually looking for what the radical groups have to offer. Those who join do so because they want to, and because they find the commitment gratifying and psychologically rewarding. Most of the radical groups disappear within a few years. They are a means by which young people emancipate themselves and find meaning in their lives.[59]

Other investigators have found that the cult experience can become confining and involuntary. Professor Margaret Thaler Singer and a colleague from the Department of Psychiatry at the University of California, Berkeley, met with one hundred young people who had entered and then left such groups as the Children of God, the Unification Church of the Rev. Sun Myung Moon, the Krishna Consciousness movement, the Divine Light Mission, and the Church of Scientology. She found

57. Ibid.
58. Ibid.
59. Ibid.

in these groups similarities to long-established and respected religious traditions and to earlier utopian ideals. Although the cults or groups were often quite different from one another, the joiners seemed to have undergone similar experiences, for example, sophisticated and effective recruitment and indoctrination procedures.[60]

Why did the youths join the religious cults? Singer says that most of those interviewed seem to have joined during periods of depression and confusion, a time when they felt that life was meaningless. The cult promised a solution to the crisis, a belief that is common among this age group. Cults supplied ready-made friendships and offered not advice, but decisions about careers, dating, sex, and marriage. The members were usually happy during their membership and "gratified to submerge their troubled selves into a selfless whole." They accepted and welcomed the indoctrination procedures that bound them closer to the group and that also removed conflicting ties or information.[61]

She also found, however, that if the member became restless or dissatisfied, escape or separation was not easy. Of the youths examined, 75 did not leave of their volition, but were removed by others, who had sought legal assistance or authority. Many were grateful for the intervention and were hoping to be rescued, she notes.[62]

A popular book about the religious cults, *Snapping*, by Flo Conway and Jim Siegelman, estimates that there are between 1,000 and 3,000 minor cults in the United States, with a combined membership of approximately 3 million. The Unification church claims 7,500 members, but the authors estimate something closer to half that number. Hare Krishna claims 10,000 members, and the Church of Scientology estimates its U.S. membership at 3.2 million (Conway and Siegelman place it closer to 25,000).[63]

As did earlier "radical" groups, such as the Mormons, Christian Scientists, and Jehovah's Witnesses, some of the modern radical groups are becoming "less doctrinaire, more moderate

60. Margaret Thaler Singer, "Coming Out of the Cults," *Psychology Today* (January, 1979): 72.
61. Ibid.
62. Ibid.
63. Ibid.

in appearance and practice, and so more acceptable to the general public."[64] Others, however, have remained both radical and controversial. Few, for example, have continued so unorthodox in theology and life-style as the followers of Bhagwan Shree Rajneesh. In 1981, the Bhagwan's disciples bought a sixty-four-thousand-acre ranch two hundred miles from Portland, Oregon. Bhagwan, which literally means "blessed one," taught philosophy at several Indian universities before beginning a career as a guru. He developed a blend of Eastern religion and pop psychology and opened an ashram in Poona, India, in 1974, where he received more than fifty thousand visitors a year. Most of these were wealthy Americans and Europeans attracted to his "encounter" and "free-love" therapy. One alumnus of Poona said that many came for sex and others for drugs. "He offered us freedom. It was wild."[65]

When India revoked the ashram's tax-exempt status in 1981 and charged the Bhagwan for back taxes, he abruptly departed for the United States on a three-month medical visa. His ranch was rezoned as a city under Oregon's land-use laws and contained six thousand of his followers. Local residents of the nearby town of Antelope left as the Rajneeshee took over and changed the name to Rajneesh, turned the general store into a restaurant, and legalized nudity in the public park. Discussing the Bhagwan, Edward Mann, a sociologist who had studied the Rajneeshee for some years, said, "He may be heating up to martyrdom so that he can go down in history as the spiritual leader of our time."[66] The departure from the United States in 1985 of the Bhagwan and many of his key lieutenants following charges of income tax evasion disrupted the colony and brought the Bhagwan infamy rather than martyrdom.

Joshua Baran, a former Zen priest who counsels dropouts from such groups, explains the phenomenon of joining as being like a rush of adrenalin. It is a liberating and exhilarating experience. You think you have the answers and everything becomes clear. It is a spiritual rush "that most people do not feel in ordinary life except in battle or in the middle of a foot-

64. Margot Slade, "New Religious Groups: Membership and Legal Battles," *Psychology Today* (January, 1979): 81.
65. Ibid.
66. "Bhagwan's Realm," *Newsweek* (December 3, 1984): 34–38.

ball field. Like a drug, you get hooked on the intensity."[67] Although most young Americans do not join cults—indeed, very few do—the cult or radical religious experience is actually not too far removed from the mainstream American life-style. The truth of the matter is, we have become a consumerist society, and religion or religious fads are one of the things we consume.

The Consumerist Religion of Tomorrow

It is not a very pretty picture, but if a person takes a truly hard look at American society and the religious environment, as has Ted Peters at the Pacific Lutheran Seminary and the Graduate Theological Union at Berkeley, it is easy to accept the notion that Americans view religion as simply another commodity. Peters believes that, as we move into the post-industrial era, our preoccupation with consuming goods and services will lead us to "commoditize religion," if we have not already done so. He believes that there is a strong trend toward treating the moral and spiritual dimensions of life as commodities to be "acquired and disposed" of according to the current whims and tastes of the shoppers in the "religious marketplace." Peters believes that we are going to be condemned to "prostitutions of the essential religious vision," which, he says, provide a sense of the transcendent unity of all things and require a sacrifice of the human ego.[68]

What will religion be like in the future? Peters believes it is going to be treated like a consumer item. Because of our wealth, he says, "we are free to consume and consume beyond the point of satiation." In fact, because it is so easy to consume material goods, we feel it necessary to go beyond material wants, to consume "personal experience." Travel is one of those experiences; religion may be another. He expects us to begin consuming religious experiences, including personal growth cults, drug-induced ecstasy, world-traveling gurus, and programs in mystical meditation. Religious entrepreneurs

67. Ibid.
68. Ted Peters, "The Future of Religion in a Post-Industrial Society," *The Futurist* (October, 1980): 21.

and even mainline denominations will begin to "pander" to the cults and advertise their "spiritual realities." He says it will all be cloaked in the noble language of personal growth, "but nevertheless the pressure will be on between now and the year 2000 to treat religious experience as a commodity for consumption."[69]

The mass media religion of the present is a signal of the coming consumerist religion of tomorrow. The electronic or televised church offers the consumer the opportunity to "dial a faith." The television preacher must sell his or her product fast. The product will have to be attractively packaged, simple, and hard-hitting in that it appeals to the known wants and desires of the consumer. "Members of the viewing public," Peters says, "will be able to sit at home and watch the religion of their choice. . . . By pushing buttons on a hand-held console, they will be able to order a book . . . or make a financial pledge." It will be, Peters says, "religion without geographical proximity, without eye-to-eye contact, without personal commitment, without fellowship. It will be religion totally at the consumer's disposal."[70]

Peters labels this kind of religious practice, "industrial narcissism," or simply another ego trip. It is not true religion, because religion requires the sacrifice of the self. Hinduism says that true liberation (Moksha) is only found when one surrenders oneself to the transcendent unity of all things (Brahman); Buddhism requires a "letting go"; and the very word *Islam* means "surrender." In Christianity, believers must take up the cross and follow. Peters sees two possible futures: one in which the consumerist religion accelerates to the point that we experience a literal cultural breakdown; and the other in which we are led to an authentic religious encounter and the understanding of the transcendent unity of all things.[71] Should the latter happen, and Peters is not too optimistic that it will, humankind will be greatly enriched.

Religious expression in America is taking two seemingly contradictory roads. On the one hand, the fundamentalist groups are growing while more liberal, mainline denomina-

69. Ibid.
70. Ibid.
71. Ibid.

tions are losing members. On the other hand, individuals appear to be more independent of religious authority and are experimenting with new radical religious groups and with personal and individual assessments of spiritual growth. The most strict and demanding denominations, such as the Southern Baptists, are growing fastest. Americans, and especially young Americans, need structure, not ambiguity. They want something solid, not something to debate. In a way, both radical groups and fundamentalist groups offer this structure and solidity.[72]

John Naisbitt, author of the best-selling *Megatrends*, believes that we are experiencing a religious revival reminiscent of the early nineteenth century, when American society was going through the transition from an agricultural to an industrial society. The environment is much the same in the transition period from the industrial to the postindustrial era. People seek structure during times of instability and change. For some, that stability means resisting change, and the fundamentalists are attractive because they represent a stark opposition to modernism. The world today, some scholars such as Gillian Peele of Oxford University believe, is not unlike that of the 1920s, when evangelism, revivalism, pietism, the holiness movements, and "traditionalism" were in vogue. In the 1920s, self-determination and prohibition were great social issues; today social causes attract many people from the religious community.[73]

Religion and Politics

Alexis de Tocqueville's observation of the strong religious atmosphere in America almost two hundred years ago is no less true today. His belief that this religious environment held strong political implications is no less true now. The social and moral upheavals of modern times have created unique political liaisons among religious groups. For example, the abortion issue has brought together fundamentalist Protestant and Roman Catholic and evangelical in a single political cause.

72. John Naisbitt, *Megatrends* (New York: Warner Books, 1982), p. 269.
73. Ibid.; Gillian Peele, *Revival and Reaction* (Oxford: Oxford University Press, 1984), pp. 92–93.

There has been a revival of religious involvement in the political arena. There has been a reconsideration of the role of religion in American life. Churches have assumed an enhanced political role.[74] Serious moral questions cannot be resolved without reference to the religious traditions of a people.

The problem is that the politicization of religion invites religious warfare. The question becomes, as Richard John Neuhaus puts it, not a question of religion but of *whose* religion, not a question of Christianity, but of *whose* Christianity. Taking religion into the public arena invites open-ended conflict and possible anarchy. But it can be no other way. A public ethic cannot be established, or re-established, unless it is informed by religiously grounded values. A ruling or decision on a question relating to ethics and morality can only be democratically legitimate if it has been examined and evaluated by the religious community. The American people, because of their deep-rooted religious environment, cannot make such decisions without reference to their religion.[75]

Neuhaus says that politics is in large part a function of culture, and at the heart of culture, particularly American culture, is religion. Religion does not refer only to established churches or doctrine, but to "all the ways we think and act and interact with respect to what we believe is ultimately true and important." It is because of this reality that many, if not most, Americans have taken offense to the notion that we are a secular society. "They feel that they were not consulted by whoever decided that this is a secular society. And they resent that; they resent it very much."[76]

Neuhaus argues that in a society such as ours, you cannot exclude religion. If you do, "the vacuum will be filled by the agent left in control of the public square, the state. In this manner, the perverse notion of the disestablishment of religion leads to the establishment of the state as church. . . . The notion of the secular state can become the prelude to totalitarianism. That is, once religion is reduced to nothing more than privatized conscience the public square has only

74. Peele, *Revival and Reaction*, pp. 92–93.
75. Richard John Neuhaus, *The Naked Public Square* (Grand Rapids, Mich.: William B. Eerdmans Publishing, 1984), p. 21.
76. Ibid., p. 27.

two actors in it—the state and the individual."[77] Religion, he says, is a mediating structure, a community that generates and transmits moral values, and most important, it is a countervailing force to the ambitions of the state.

In part for that reason, the Christian and Jewish traditions in America are not just peripherally or accidentally concerned about politics, they are essentially and intentionally concerned. A public political ethic requires discussion of religious visions of "good" and "justice" because that is the way most Americans perceive good and justice. In an August, 1984, address, President Ronald Reagan clearly enunciated this union of religion and politics: "I believe that faith and religion play a critical role in the political life of our nation, and always have, and that the church—and by that I mean all churches, all denominations—has a strong influence on the state, and this has worked to our benefit as a nation."[78] Not unexpectedly, President Reagan was immediately attacked and criticized for rewriting the Constitution and for rejecting the tradition of the separation of church and state.

But columnist Allan C. Brownfeld, among others, believes that those who criticize the concept that Americans are a "nation under God" do not understand the American tradition. Reverence for God has been a part of the public life of Americans since they arrived. The Declaration of Independence acknowledges God in four different places, and the Constitution specifically recognizes the freedom of religion, as well as the separation of church and state. The United States is a nation "with the soul of a church," G. K. Chesterton said. It is not and never has been the secular society that some seem to seek.[79]

Americans of all ages remain deeply committed to religious values. That commitment is being expressed in more varied ways than ever before. The casual observer might well believe that Americans are the least likely "other worldly" people on

---

77. Ibid.
78. Allan C. Brownfeld, "Religion, Politics: The Myth of America as a Secular Society," *Manchester [N.H.] Union Leader* (October 21, 1984); Harvey Cox, "Putting God Back into Politics," *New York Times Book Review* (August 26, 1984): 11.
79. Brownfeld, "Religion, Politics," p. 22.

earth and are far more interested in the here and now than in the hereafter. But a closer look, no matter in what time or in what place, argues that materialistic Americans have remained a God-fearing people, despite modernization, secularization, urbanization, and industrialization.[80]

There will likely be visible changes in the structures of the traditional churches, and many new structures and religious manifestations in the future. Decentralization and individualism will be characteristic of religious institutions, perhaps even to the point of a form of anarchy. Religion may well become more of a mosaic of "shifting issues, causes, episodes, and groups." Certainly there is good evidence of that now. But the apparent disintegration will actually generate a new energy and spirituality. This new energy and spirituality can help fashion a civilization with great material accomplishments and discoveries, and one equally full in the things of the spirit.[81] The forms may change, and the individual's relationship to organized churches may differ. The place of religion in American society, however, will not be diminished, but if anything, will grow larger.

80. "Friday Night Fervor Fills D.C. Synagogue," *Washington Times* (October 4, 1984).

81. "The Year Things Change," p. 51; and Hugh Meyers, "Christianity in the Coming Decades: The Search for Faith in a Secular World," *The Futurist* (June, 1979): 165.

CHAPTER FOUR

Notes on the American System of Education

The American system of universal public education remains a unique social experience. Religion and the concept of public education are closely tied to the cultural mores of the American people. Education was popularly espoused in the colonies and in the young republic not only as a means to train the citizenry in self-government, but as an opportunity to make it easier for the evangelical Protestant churches to spread the gospel. It was important that every soul have the opportunity and the ability to read the Bible. Education also met the growing needs of the mercantile and then of the industrial interests in developing a source of literate clerks, accountants, and managers for business. By the Civil War, the massive ranks of the American farmer had also begun to call for the expansion of higher levels of public education to enhance their opportunities. Despite what seems to have been a very widespread, if not universal, demand for free public education, the achievement of a successful system of public education at the lower or higher levels has not been rapid or easy. In the 1980s, there remains considerable doubt about the accomplishments of the American educational system.

The considerable criticism of the system is nothing new, and it is perhaps useful to put current discontent into a broader context. That astute observer of the early nineteenth century American scene, Alexis de Tocqueville, provides some useful perspective for understanding what American education is about. Writing in the 1830s, he observed that America as of that time had produced "very few writers of distinction . . . no great historians and not a single eminent poet." There were towns of "second-rate importance in Europe," he said, that published more literary works annually than the twenty-four American states published put together.[1]

Nevertheless, de Tocqueville said, Americans were not ignorant. On the contrary, the system of education he found to be unique and rather astonishing. An observer, he said, would find very few "learned" Americans, but, on the other hand, if an observer were looking for the ignorant, they would not be found either. "The American people will appear to be the most enlightened in the world."[2] In New England, de Tocqueville said, every citizen was taught the basic notions of human knowledge—and the doctrines and evidences of religion, "the history of the country, and the leading features of the Constitution." It was extremely rare to find a person "imperfectly acquainted with all these things, and a person wholly ignorant of them is sort of a phenomenon."[3] Even the most remote backwoodsman living in a miserable log hut de Tocqueville discovered to be a remarkably enlightened person: "He wears the dress and speaks the language of cities; he is acquainted with the past, curious about the future, and ready for argument about the present; he is, in short, a highly civilized being who consents for a time to inhabit the backwoods, and who penetrates into the wilds of the New World with the Bible, an axe, and some newspapers."[4] Education, concluded this Old World visitor to the New, contributed powerfully to the support of democracy, and the instruction that "enlightened the understanding" was not separated from "the moral education which amends the heart."[5]

De Tocqueville viewed the educational setting before Horace Mann's strong imprint. Against strong opposition from propertied interests and the sectarian monopoly of education, Horace Mann of Massachusetts and Henry Barnard of Con-

1. Alexis de Tocqueville, *Democracy in America*, ed. Phillip Bradley from the 1835 Henry Reeve edition, vol. 1 (New York: Alfred A. Knopf, 1945), pp. 326–27.
2. Ibid., p. 327.
3. Ibid.
4. Ibid., p. 328.
5. Ibid., p. 329.

necticut led the reform movement that took education into the public domain as never before. (Mann, incidentally, insisted that a moral regeneration was necessary to preserve the "Christian republic" and that education required public, not just private or parochial support.)[6] Mann and the educational reformers of the 1830s and 1840s, to be sure, followed a precedent established during the days of the early republic. The Northwest Ordinance, for example, approved by the Congress under the Articles of Confederation, reserved every sixteenth section of the public lands for education. Virginia, under the leadership of its governor, Thomas Jefferson, established operating systems of public education at the lower and higher levels prior to the adoption of the Constitution. Mann's victories for public education in the northern states, unfortunately, did not extend to most of those that would soon become identified as the South.

Although many states had public institutions of higher education before the Civil War, higher education remained largely the function of sectarian or private institutions. The Morrill Land Grant College Act of 1862 was a catalyst in expanding college-level public education, in part because it brought into focus the need for "practical training" for the American citizenry, as opposed to training in literature, the arts, and a life of leisure, which the classical studies of the time were said to provide. The agricultural and mechanical colleges created under the Morrill Act offered scientific and industrial training to the people without excluding the liberal arts, and including a provision for military training.[7] Education at all levels continued on an erratic and difficult course throughout the nineteenth century. That course has changed little in the twentieth century.

Perhaps today as at no time since the reform era of Horace Mann has the American system of education been in the throes of such agonizing reappraisal and change. Just as the

6. See Thomas Jefferson, "A Bill for the More General Diffusion of Knowledge," and Horace Mann, "10th (1846) and 12th (1848) Annual Reports to the Massachusetts Board of Education," in James William Noll and Sam P. Kelly, eds., *Foundations of Education in America: An Anthology of Major Thoughts and Significant Actions* (New York: Harper and Row, 1970), pp. 143–47, 209–15.

7. "The Morrill Act of 1862," in Noll and Kelly, *Foundations of Education*, pp. 253–54.

age of humanitarian reforms recalled great social change and marked the beginning of the abolition and women's rights movements, so do the educational changes occurring now in the context of the civil rights movements and substantive economic changes. Rapid and unexpected change has undermined the strength of the educational superstructure or bureaucracy. Greater flexibility of institutions is required to meet the demands of modern education, which must now, it seems, teach one how to develop oneself and to adapt to changing realities.[8]

In a very real sense, the objectives of modern education are not unlike traditional educational goals. Education is a process of self-development. It may be that we have not really changed our goals so much as missed those goals through some rather well-meaning but misguided efforts to serve education on a platter without giving the recipient instruction in how and what to consume from the platter. We give Johnny thousands of books and teachers educated in the best colleges and universities we can build, but still the popular lament is "Johnny can't read!"

Johnny Can't Read

A 1979 federal study estimated that 13 percent of the nation's seventeen-year-olds are "functionally illiterate." In college after college, including the elite universities, more than 30 percent of the entering freshmen now have serious problems in reading, writing, and mathematics.[9] A recent survey of eight hundred businesses in the United States indicates that one-third of them felt it necessary to provide their employees with remedial education in the three R's—reading, writing, and arithmetic. A Continental Illinois Bank officer informed a reporter that "more and more of the applicants whom we're seeing straight out of school can't write a complete sentence."[10] For many years educators and administrators have claimed that smaller classes, better salaries, and more money for education would solve the problems. Over the past decades the United

8. Orville Freeman and William Person, "Multinational Corporations: Hope for the Poorest Nations," *The Futurist* (December, 1980).
9. Solveig Eggerz, "Why Our Public Schools Are Failing," *America's Future* (1982).
10. Ibid.

States has poured more money into education. But the teaching, or at least the results, have failed to improve; indeed, there are continuing declines in those abilities measured by the standardized tests.

Public expenditure on education in the United States per inhabitant is twice that of Europe and three times as large as that of the Soviet Union. Yet in competitive examinations taken by students of the industrialized countries, Americans score at or near the bottom. Scholastic Aptitude Examination (SAT) scores peaked in the 1962–1963 school year, with a national average of 478 in the verbal test and 502 in mathematics. Scores have dwindled since. The decline at times has seemed precipitous.[11]

Solveig Eggerz, author of "Why Our Public Schools Are Failing," identifies many symptoms of this suspected failure. Eggerz points to a National Science Foundation study that warns that America is headed toward "scientific and technological illiteracy." Public school students have a very high dropout rate in science and mathematics, and less than one-third of the high-school graduates ever complete courses in chemistry, physics, or trigonometry. A survey by the National Association of Educational Progress found that 47 percent of all seventeen-year-olds tested did not know that each state had two U.S. senators, and about one-third believed that the president appointed the members of Congress. When the Internal Revenue Service revised the income tax forms in 1981, the reading level was set at the ninth grade, two grade levels lower than earlier forms. The language is still widely criticized for being complicated and obscure.[12]

This, of course, is only a small sampling of the problems that have begun to appear in the American system of education. The point is, Johnny cannot read as well as he used to be able to read, nor write, nor do his arithmetic. What's the problem? Is Johnny really less bright? Are teachers failing in their teaching? Are we in some way scrimping on education? Are our legislators and the local school boards failing in their duties? What are the causes for the "decline" in education, and what can we expect?

11. Ibid.
12. Ibid.

Why Can't Johnny Read?

There are about as many explanations for the problems in education as there are educators and observers. The high mobility of American society, school population pressures that have become almost overwhelming, poorly or inadequately trained teachers, insufficient funding, changing demography, the social and educational upheavals brought on by the civil rights legislation and court decisions of the 1950s and 1960s, the explosion of knowledge and information, and the "lack of discipline" in the schools and in the home are all acknowledged as contributing to the "problems" in education.

Teachers are quick, and rightfully so, to point to the lack of discipline, even violence in the public schools as a serious deterrent to good teaching. A report by the National Institute of Education found that 282,000 students were attacked in a recent year. Another 7.5 million were robbed. Eighty-five percent of all junior high and senior high school students in the big cities missed one day of school a month out of fear that they would be attacked or robbed. In Miami a twenty-four-year-old science teacher was stabbed to death while trying to evict a teenage dropout. Shootings have occurred on the school grounds and in school cafeterias. Teachers have been shot and beaten by angry students. One study indicates that in a typical month 5,200 teachers are physically assaulted, 1,000 of whom require medical attention. An estimated one-half of all public school teachers are abused by gesture or remarks each month.[13]

Why have these things happened? Clearly they are in part only a symptom in the apparent breakdown of "law and order" in the broader social context. One contributing factor, school administrators think, is the series of court decisions that, in protecting the rights of the student, have made it virtually impossible to remove disciplinary problems from the classroom. In areas where minority students are found to be disproportionately responsible for discipline problems, efforts to impose corrective measures often produce charges of discrimi-

13. Ibid.

nation.[14] Students are given the authority under court precedent, or sometimes simple expediency, to challenge teachers
and administrators for disciplinary actions. The result has been
to create a "protected class" of student who thrives on disrup-
tion and is basically immune from retaliation. Under the laws
of most states, students are required to attend class until at
least age sixteen, whether they or their parents desire it or
not. Schools cannot impose discipline, nor can they remove
offenders from the classroom.[15]

As educators properly point out, the disintegration of discipline in the schools reflects the same symptoms throughout society. Political assassinations, growing crime on the
street against persons and property, the burning of draft cards,
marches, strikes, and violent protest or riot could be easily
misinterpreted by the average youth and certainly set no model
for discipline and respect for authority. The decline of the family as a disciplining structure and, indeed, the growing affluence of Americans have contributed to the problems in the
classroom. Gordon Ampach, commissioner of education for
New York State, declares that "although schools have particular responsibilities to assist children in developing self-
discipline and nurturing civic responsibility, the family must
provide a child with his or her first and continuing experience
with self-restraint."[16] In a very real sense, the teachers and the
educational system have had greater burdens imposed on them
because of the changes in family and society and simple demographic changes.

Not too long ago, about one-half of the American people
were under the age of twenty-five and most were enrolled in
secondary schools or colleges. Moreover, the mix of students
had changed considerably from the pre–World War II days. Immigration is presumed by most to have peaked in the decade
between 1900 and 1910, when almost 9 million legal immigrants
arrived in the United States. Immigration reached 2.5 million
in the fifties, 3.2 million in the sixties, and 4.5 million in the
seventies. The number of illegal immigrants in the correspond-

14. Ibid.
15. Ibid.
16. Ibid.

ing decades is thought by some to have almost matched the legal immigration. The result was a new burden on the school system, not only in numbers, but often in language and ethnic or cultural communication.[17] The rise in "functional illiteracy" has been in part a product of this new immigration.

Immigration will continue to have some impact on the school system. The new immigration has affected the ethnic composition of student enrollments and will have a greater effect in the future. In 1980, the American population included 79 percent white (non-Hispanic), 12 percent black, 7 percent Hispanic, and 2 percent Asian (and other). Projections indicate that at the end of the next hundred years, given the current immigration levels and birth rates of ethnic groups, the U.S. population will comprise 10 percent Asian, 16 percent each of black and Hispanic, and 59 percent white (non-Hispanic).[18]

The new immigrants are changing the cultural milieu of the American people. Today's new arrivals are from Latin America and, to a lesser extent, Asia and the Caribbean. From 1960 to 1980, the largest number of immigrants came from Cuba, with 473,000 arrivals. The Philippines were second with 453,000, followed in order by Korea (302,000), the Dominican Republic (241,000), India (191,000), Vietnam (177,000), and Colombia (149,000). The number of illegal immigrants in the same time period is estimated as high as 5 million, with most of these from Latin America.[19]

The new immigration could mean that an additional thirty-five million people will be added to the total population by the year 2000, if the present levels continue. It does mean that the United States has already been enriched by "a mosaic of exotic languages, faces, costumes, customs, restaurants and religions."[20] Immigration will also have significant economic import, indeed, is having that impact now. Legal immigration even now accounts for about one-fourth of total population growth. Julian Simon at the University of Maryland suggests that, particularly in view of the declining birth rate of resi-

17. Ben Wattenberg, *The Good News Is the Bad News Is Wrong* (New York: Simon and Schuster, 1984), p. 75.

18. Ibid., p. 76.

19. Ibid.

20. Gene I. Maeroff, "Religious Studies Are Thinning," *New York Times* (Oct. 23, 1984), C1, C9.

dent populations, the new immigrants will become the workers, consumers, entrepreneurs, and taxpayers who invigorate
the economy. "This country needs more, not fewer, immigrants. The U.S. birthrate is low and our future work force is
shrinking. By opening our doors we will not only do good but
the evidence indicates we will also do well."[21] The educational
system will have the primary role of educating and training
the immigrant, a role it has been ill-prepared to accept in the
recent past.

It would seem that the educational processes have served
poorly not only the newly arrived Americans but also those
who were already residents. The United States spent 6.8 percent of its GNP in 1980–1981 (or two hundred billion dollars)
on education, double the amount spent in 1949–1950 and more
per capita and in total than any other country in the world.
Yet, in an academic competency test comparing American
sixth graders with their counterparts in seven other industrialized countries, American children in 1983 ranked *last* in mathematics and little better in science and geography.[22]

The test was sponsored by the *Dallas Times-Herald* and
developed by four prominent educators. It was administered
to sixth-grade students in Australia, Canada, England, France,
Japan, Sweden, Switzerland, and the United States. The participating schools were rated average in each of their respec-
tive countries. The American students attended two Dallas,
Texas, elementary schools whose pupils ranked average or
above on the Iowa Test of Basic Skills, which is the most widely
used standardized test of math and reading comprehension.
The results were described as "alarming" by Glenn Seaborg,
the Nobel Prize-winning scientist who helped direct the science portion of the test, and "embarrassing" by Stephen Wil-
loughby, president of the National Council of Teachers of
Mathematics, who developed the math questions.[23]

The traditional response to perceived problems in educa-

21. Ibid.
22. Leon F. Bouvier and Cary B. Davis, *The Future Racial Composition
of the United States* (Washington, D.C.: Demographic Information Service
Center of Population Reference Bureau, August, 1982).
23. Allan C. Brownfeld, "More Funds Do Not a School Make, nor a Higher
Salary an Instructor," syndicated column distributed by Free Press International News Service, October 15, 1984.

tion is to spend more money. Yet, the United States is spending far more per capita than the countries whose students outperform our own. Roger Freeman of the Hoover Institution estimates American educational expenditures at two hundred billion dollars per year, or roughly 7.5 percent of the GNP, as compared to a spending level of 4.1 percent for the Soviet Union. Approximately 30 percent of the American population is involved in education. There are about 59 million students and 6.6 million employees in the American system of education, which by almost any measurement, makes it the nation's biggest business.[24]

In 1975, public expenditures on education per inhabitant in North America were twice those of Europe, and three times as high as in the Soviet Union. The United States has increased financial support (in constant dollars) and staff to two or three times the increase in numbers of students during the past twenty-five years. There is, however, little evidence that there is a cost-quality relationship in the schools.[25]

Roger Freeman's study of education indicates that as expenditures per student increased and class sizes were being reduced, learning levels were falling. The mean scores on the college board tests "have been declining dramatically for two decades," and even the achievement levels of the most gifted students are dwindling because these students are not being challenged with a sufficiently demanding curriculum or rigorous grading standards.[26]

A recent comparative study done at the University of Michigan of students in Japan, Taiwan, and the United States indicates that the achievement of American schoolchildren in reading and mathematics is behind that of students in Japan and Taiwan, and that the deficiency seems to appear almost from the first day of school. The surveyors found that a plausible explanation is simply that American students spend less time in school, do less homework, and, when they are in class, are more likely to be engaged in "academically irrelevant" activities.[27]

Most public schools systems have practiced "social promo-

24. Ibid.
25. Ibid.
26. Ibid.
27. Ibid.

tion," which means that students are moved from one grade to the next even though they may not have mastered any body of material. For most, graduation from high school comes almost automatically at age eighteen. Moreover, grades will almost inevitably indicate that students have performed satisfactory work.

What is applicable to the students is no less applicable to the teacher. The tendency has been for teachers to receive tenure and regular salary increases based on a formula using time as the primary basis, rather than merit or achievement. The result is that the American system of education offers no incentive to teach, and no incentive to learn.[28] There is evidence that this is changing and, indeed, has never been characteristic of all school systems. In fact, that may be one of the problems with the public schools, that in a time of high social mobility, with many students moving from one school to another, the schools are very uneven in their quality, standards, and curricula, particularly between the states.

Although other states and school systems have imposed more rigorous standards, action by Texas is symptomatic of the changing attitudes and requirements. Texas imposed a controversial "no pass, no play" rule, which requires secondary students participating in extracurricular activities to pass all courses in which they are enrolled, or be disqualified from participation for the next six weeks. The courses that most students failed during the first six weeks of the program in the fall of 1985 were English, history, and mathematics. Students must also pass a qualifying examination to indicate that they meet the standards required for graduation before receiving a diploma. Teachers must pass a qualifying examination to be certified to teach. Teachers are also rated according to their teaching skills, with master teacher certification for those who qualify. In addition, salary increments are especially designed for those who are expert teachers.[29] Initiated by a special study group headed by businessman H. Ross Perot, the new procedures are at this writing still on trial and still controversial, but the message has come through rather strongly

28. Ibid.
29. Select Committee on Public Education, "Recommendations," Austin, Texas, April 19, 1984, pp. 1–44.

that students, faculty, parents, and legislators want to get serious about educating Johnny.

The Perot Commission recognized, as have other educators and public officials, that quality is not necessarily directly related to money spent. Indeed, new courses in the school curriculum have most often been in nonacademic subjects, subjects that are more expensive to teach on a unit basis. Sex education, driver training, bachelor living, and computer literacy cost considerably more per capita to teach than do English, history, and mathematics.

In *The Literacy Hoax*, Paul Copperman compared the current typical high-school English curriculum with one from the early 1960s. In the 1960s, the mandatory sequence at a suburban California high school included a year of composition, a year of American literature, and a year of British literature. Senior English included one-semester options such as creative writing, journalism, public speaking, debating, classical literature, advanced composition, or poetry. Today the survey courses are no longer required and the student can choose from a variety of nonrigorous courses. At the same suburban high school students are now required to take two mandatory semesters of English in the ninth grade and one in the first semester of the tenth grade. They are also required to take three additional semesters of nonspecified English courses during their last two and one-half years of school. The options include those available in 1960, plus American literature, tutoring, philosophy, satire, semantics, Shakespeare, sports literature, communications, drama, the hero in literature, popular culture, advanced composition, mass media, mythology and folklore, survey of the novel, the short story, Afro-American literature, and survival English. In the 1960s, the student was required to take eight semesters of English, with two elective semesters; currently the student is required to take six semesters of English with three of them elective, and the electives have proliferated.

This is not to say that courses in science fiction or folklore are bad. It does indicate, however, that instruction in what might be termed the "basics" has been reduced. The public schools and, indeed, the universities, have tended to abandon the more traditional or serious academic courses to offer a current nonacademic smorgasbord of electives that are de-

scribed as "pandering to students who have increasingly abandoned academic and vocational studies for 'general track'
courses like 'Training for Adulthood.'"[30]

Our schools have been flooded with innovative, experimen-
tal programs and curricula. Not all have been bad, but some
have. But both the good and the bad have tended to come and
go with the seasons, leaving the student little but confusion
and a real deficiency in basic instruction. In part, federal funding, which was regarded as the answer to the problem of education in the 1960s, is to blame for the problem in education
in the 1980s. Much of the federally funded innovation occurs
under Title I of the Elementary and Secondary Education Act,
which among other things, provides "compensatory" funding
for the education of deprived youngsters. Federal funds have
most often been used to purchase expensive equipment, in-
dividualized learning packets, and to develop learning centers
and hire teacher aides. The long-term result has been to diminish the role of the teacher and make that person a "facili-
tator" of education rather than an instructor. The proliferation of paraprofessionals and "outside" specialists also tends
to diminish the teaching role of the teacher. Finally, the simple proliferation of teaching materials and texts, which is part
of the information explosion, contributes to some confusion
in the classroom and in the learning processes. Materials are
hardly mastered before new ones, sometimes diametrically different, such as "phonics" in reading, or "new math" in mathematics, take their place. We are literally afloat in a sea of new
educational opportunities and information.[31]

Under federally funded programs, a child may be exposed
to as many as five basic reading programs in his or her first
six years of school. In many school districts, programs are
changed every two or three years.[32] If a child moves from one
school district to another, or to another state, the change of
pace or program is likely to be acute in almost every instance.
Almost all families will make major geographic moves during a child's precollege school career.

Families are responding to the problems in the public

30. Eggerz, "Why Our Public Schools Are Failing," pp. 1–173.
31. Ibid.
32. Ibid.

schools in part by moving their children to private schools, which are being established in record numbers. The National Association of Independent Schools reports that one new school is being started every ten days. Christian fundamentalist schools are being opened at the fastest pace. Boarding schools, out of favor with the American public in recent decades, have come back into vogue. Boarding school applications have jumped by 25 percent since 1977. In 1980, about 5.1 million students were attending private schools in the United States.[33]

In a 1982 Gallup poll, Americans reaffirmed their belief in the importance of education, but one-half of those canvassed said they would prefer sending their children to private schools if they could afford to do so. Curiously, according to Robert Recerski, the principal of Arlington Baptist School in Baltimore, the "largest single bloc of parents by profession who send their kids to Christian schools" is the public school administrators and teachers. These people, who are most knowledgeable, say that the private school offers more discipline and a better academic environment.

Not only the well-to-do send their children to private schools. In 1980, it was estimated that 60 percent of the parents whose children attended private schools earned less than twenty thousand dollars per year. In New York City, black educators estimate there are nearly one hundred black-operated private schools, with many of the students coming from relatively low-income families.[34]

The search to solve current problems in education has led to a profitable examination of those qualities that make some schools successful. Child psychiatrist Michael Rutter, for example, found that students from the poorer neighborhoods of London achieved more if they were in academically rigorous schools with an orderly environment. They also learned more if their teachers assigned and checked homework on a regular basis and were strong instructors in the classroom. Other analyses indicate that the better students come from schools where the principals are active leaders, the schools are orderly and emphasize basic skills, and the teachers have high expec-

33. Ibid.
34. Ibid.

tations for all of their students. Schools must have a strong academic focus. Higher levels of funding do not necessarily produce academic achievement, nor do they preclude achievement. The important thing in the educational process, as one journalist summarized, is that the only two real ingredients in education are time and people. To the degree that you mobilize and focus on these resources, you have achievement.[35]

Educators and the general public have always been intrigued that some of our best writers, scientists, and politicians are products of the one-room schoolhouse. There the academic environment was truly honed to its basic ingredients—time and people. Equipment and accoutrements, including texts, were often nonexistent. The teacher worked with students at every level, but perhaps more important, the students were required to interact with each other and with the teacher. Older students tutored the younger, and in a way, each student contributed to the education of the others. More than small class size was involved in the one-room school education. There was greater concentration per unit of time on basic information.

Private schools have had greater success than the public in re-establishing the one-room school environment, with its discipline and concentration on subject matter. In good measure, this success has been a product of size, but it is also a result of parental concern and moral support. Students are there because they want to be educated, or at least their parents want them to be educated. The movement from public schools to private is likely to continue for those who can afford it. A key to the continuation of this movement will be the tuition tax credits being considered in Congress and the response of the public schools to the problems being complained about by parents and educators.

The tuition tax credit proposals currently under consideration would permit parents who send their children to nonpublic schools to deduct 50 percent of tuition costs, up to five hundred dollars annually, from their federal tax liability. The measure, or one similar, would make private schools accessible to many more students and would likely create additional incentives for public school systems to initiate educa-

35. Ibid.

tional reforms. Walter Williams, a black economist at George Mason University, argues that a tuition tax credit will create better opportunities for students who are often now processed out of the public schools and remain illiterate. They are being served up "a grossly fraudulent education." These children, black and white alike, will be major beneficiaries of a tuition tax credit. It would give them access to a better education than they can currently receive, or at least offer options that they do not now have.[36]

One response to current problems in education has been the rise of the self-help movement. Parental involvement and activity in the schools have increased, sometimes to the irritation of the teachers and administrators, who resent being told what to do by nonprofessionals. Some parents are directing their children, when they can afford it, to the private schools. But some, in a more radical movement, have determined upon "alternative" schools and attempts to move the educational process from the schools into the home, sometimes as a supplement to the public school curriculum or, in more extreme cases, as a challenge to the compulsory education laws, which require public or private school enrollment.

Alternative schools of the 1960s and 1970s assumed a variety of forms and purposes and often followed the patterns or beliefs of their progenitors. Most tended to have a religious or cult base. But the alternative education movement of more recent years stresses self-instruction at home, often with the aid of sophisticated computer equipment connected by modem to educational channels or packages in a mainframe computer. One former public school educator and reformer, John Holt, estimated some years ago that ten thousand families were educating their children at home and believes it could now be as high as one million. He produces a bimonthly magazine, *Growing without Schooling*, for parents who have removed or want to remove their children from public or private schools and have them learn at home.[37]

Home schooling is not simply a radical or "lunatic fringe" movement. Raymond S. Moore, a developmental psychologist,

36. Ibid.
37. John Naisbitt, *Megatrends* (New York: Warner Books, 1982), pp. 157–58.

former principal, school superintendent, and college president, and a White House advisor, believes that the home-schooling movement is the "movement of the decade." It is growing very fast and is critical in the revolutionary changes under way in education. The movement is spreading so fast, he says, that, whereas there were only a smattering of families involved a few years ago, you now find many communities where forty or fifty parents meet regularly to plan or develop their education-at-home programs. He said that he recently spoke to a group of parents in his tiny community of Washougal, Washington, expecting to have only fifteen or so present, but more than one hundred parents attended. There are, he said, an estimated fifteen thousand to twenty thousand students being taught at home in Washington State.[38]

The rationale for home schooling can in part be attributed to the idea that the more a young student grows in an adult environment, the greater the propensity for the student to fully develop his or her intellectual capacities, and the stronger will be the character and personality of the individual. Harold Mc-Curdy, a distinguished psychologist at the University of North Carolina, says that the development of intellectual genius is derived from the experience of children spending most of their time with adults and very little of their time with other children. The assembling of large numbers of children together for long periods of time is not conducive to intellectual growth, he says.[39]

An analysis of over one thousand schools by John Goodland, the graduate dean at the University of California, Los Angeles, showed that the average amount of time spent in person-to-person responses between teachers and students was seven minutes in a school day. In a typical class of twenty-five to thirty students, if a teacher makes a direct response to questions for a total of only seven minutes a day, the individual student will very infrequently be spoken to. If the child is aggressive, or misbehaves, he or she might receive a greater portion of the teacher's personal attention, whereas at home, for

38. "Interview with Dr. Raymond Moore," *Human Events* (September 15, 1984), pp. 12–14, 19.
   39. Ibid.

example, the child can expect hundreds of direct responses from a parent each day. The home, in other words, is an adult environment that can most rapidly nurture the intellect of the child.[40] This kind of thinking supports the education-at-home movement. A counterpoint to that rationale, however, is that an education at home will often suffer from inadequate (and untrained) learning resources, and the child will fail to develop the social skills that make the intellect a more useful and effective tool.

A by-product of the education-at-home movement is that the schools have begun to solve some of the problems that have developed. Within the past few years, forty states have increased the number of basic academic courses required for graduation. Thirty-two have changed the curriculum and adopted improved procedures for choosing textbooks. Twenty-four states have lengthened the school day or reduced the amount of nonacademic time within the school day. Forty-two states have strengthened the requirements for training and certification of new teachers. Twelve states, including Texas, Florida, California, and Tennessee, have related raises to merit and achievement in teaching, or to "master teaching" programs. Most important, there has been a distinct shift in educating educators — away from the stress on process or procedures and methods to subject-matter competency.[41] An algebra or history teacher, for example, may need additional training in the subject he or she is assigned to teach.

Alternative education modes and learning-at-home programs are finding important applications outside of the traditional secondary school or college systems. A new clientele for "continuing education" has developed within the past few decades and is growing at an enormous rate. Adult and older Americans are finding that education can, and should be, a continuing process. In a time of fast-changing technology and rapid information flow, the consumption and utilization of that technology and information requires a continuation of the learning process. Although we have always "learned by ex-

40. Ibid.
41. Edward B. Fiske, "Concern over Schools Spurs Extensive Efforts at Reform," New York Times (December 9, 1984).

perience," modern life requires the more formal consumption of information.

Continuing Education

Education is becoming a lifetime enterprise. Institutions of higher education are devoting more energy to continuing education programs for people who need to bolster job skills or prepare for a career switch. Many people in fast-changing technical fields, such as computer science and engineering, medicine, chemistry, and biology, require constant updating in their specialties. Business, banking, and marketing specialists are equally affected by the information explosion. "Engineers now find that their education really starts to lose its edge about every five years," claims Glen Martin, who heads a continuing education committee for the National Society of Professional Engineers. An engineer's knowledge is either made obsolete or incorporated into computers every ten years.[42]

Know-how or technology becomes obsolete in so many fields so rapidly that formal job retraining programs are becoming commonplace. It may well be that in the future most persons educated in a technical specialty may anticipate schooling or retooling on a regular basis, or be unable to remain in that specialty and retrain for other careers. Most large corporations maintain education and training programs, not only for re-educating older employees, but for providing the recent high-school or college graduate the special skills needed by the company.

One form of continuing education that has particularly helped solve the "functional illiteracy" problem of adult immigrants and those Americans who were unable to finish high school for one reason or another is adult basic education programs. These offer adults formal classes in basic information such as reading, writing, history, and arithmetic. Students in such courses may earn continuing education units or high-school equivalency certification.

Older Americans are also finding continuing education programs increasingly attractive. Continuing education classes

42. Ibid.

can offer instruction, for example, in the creative use of leisure time, or more important, can keep older citizens abreast of current information in any area they find significant — including basic technological changes, economic and business conditions, and literature — all of which have a direct impact on the quality of life at any age.

Business executives and older Americans are also finding the computer a useful mechanism for continuing education at home. Through the home computer Americans may have access to information that might otherwise be inaccessible, even in a formal classroom setting. It is possible that the microcomputer "will replace the telephone as the predominant means of interpersonal and group communications."[43] The computer not only is aiding and abetting the knowledge explosion, but it offers a mechanism for the distribution and absorption of that information. Indeed, home working and at-home education could become synonymous activities of the postindustrial age.

Women have particularly benefited from the continuing education movement. More women than ever before are completing high-school studies, and more than ever are enrolling in and completing university and postgraduate degrees. Those women already in the work force or at home are returning to their studies in greater numbers to complete the education they left unfinished. From 1970 to 1977, the number of women in blue-collar jobs doubled as women obtained new skills through various educational and training programs. More married women than ever before are now in the labor force, 53 percent in 1982, compared to only 17 percent in 1940. The number of women in professional positions — medicine, law, engineering, and the sciences — has risen dramatically in just the last decade. Today, half of the students enrolled in college are women, compared to only one-third a generation ago.[44]

More women, more adults, more older Americans, and a more diverse ethnic mix will reflect the changing composite of students in educational environments in the future. The environments themselves will also be more diverse. There are

43. *U.S. News and World Report* (March 19, 1984): 42–43.
44. Wattenberg, *The Good News*, pp. 182–83.

likely to be more private and parochial schools. There will be more home-schooling situations for young people but perhaps more especially for adults and senior citizens. Larger businesses will use more education and retraining programs. But it is likely that the major role of education will continue to be exercised by the public school systems on both the secondary and college levels. Colleges and universities, both public and private, can likely anticipate greater pressures on technical programs, particularly for re-education and retraining purposes. One-year retooling or re-education programs might become important adjuncts to the conventional college curriculum. College, and particularly graduate school, enrollments should continue to grow under the necessities of the "knowledge explosion."

A Nation at Risk

A special federal study completed in 1983 has provided considerable impetus to the "back to the basics" movement in the public schools. It has fueled efforts to restore and maintain quality in instructional programs. Since the days of Horace Mann, there have been calls to restore, reinvigorate, or redirect the nation's educational efforts. It is this constant infusion of concern and new ideas that gives the American system of education its vitality and meaning.

A now-classic work by Alfred North Whitehead in 1929 cautioned that in the history of education one of the most striking phenomena is that schools can be "alive with the ferment of genius" in one epoch, but in succeeding generations exhibit merely "pedantry and routine." The reason for this, he said, is that schools become "overladen with inert ideas. Education with inert ideas is not only useless: it is, above all things, harmful."[45] Whitehead went on to advise that there were two great educational commandments: "Do not teach too many subjects," and "What you teach, teach thoroughly."[46] That would seem to be good advice for all times.

The sometimes controversial but very respected Admiral

---

45. Noll and Kelly, *Foundations of Education*, p. 326.
46. Ibid.

Hyman G. Rickover published a book in 1963 entitled *American Education: A National Failure*. Rickover, father of the nuclear navy, appeared frequently before congressional committees urging reform and action to improve American educational standards at every level. He advised Congress, "I do not wish to deprecate the importance of high moral standards, of good character, of kindliness, of humaneness, of ability to get along well with fellow citizens—there are innumerable virtues I should like to see inculcated in American youth. But the one thing which I believe will be of the greatest importance for the future of our Nation and the free world, the one *indispensable* thing, is to bring all our children to markedly higher intellectual levels."[47] Rickover urged the adoption of federal guidelines, standards, and assistance for secondary and higher education. Many others were urging congressional action on enhancing educational opportunities for all Americans.

The result was the passage in 1965 of three important acts that have resulted in enormous federal expenditures on all levels of education. The Elementary and Secondary Education Act was designed to "strengthen and improve educational quality and educational opportunities in the Nation's elementary and secondary schools." The act included special financial assistance to schools for the education of children of low-income families, grants to schools for library resources and instructional materials, and funds for special educational centers and services, as well as grants to strengthen state departments of education.[48]

The National Arts and Humanities Foundation Act created two federally funded foundations or agencies, including the National Endowment for the Arts and the National Endowment for the Humanities. Both provide direct support for artists, musicians, and scholars under a variety of grant programs. The Higher Education Act provided funding for continuing education programs, college library assistance, strengthening or development grants for academic programs, student assistance and loan programs, and funds for equipment. It also

47. H. G. Rickover, *American Education: A National Failure* (E. P. Dutton and Co., 1963), reprinted in Noll and Kelly, *Foundations of Education*, p. 409.

48. See Noll and Kelly, *Foundations of Education*, pp. 480–83.

called for the creation of an advisory council on quality teacher preparation.[49]

The three acts resulted in large sums of federal money going into public education, which had been almost the exclusive responsibility of state and local governments. The acts did provide for more equal educational opportunities and created new educational opportunities for people who otherwise might not have had them. They began to impose a greater degree of uniformity or standardization on education throughout the states, but they clearly did not solve the problems of education and, inadvertently, may have created a few.

Nevertheless, "education" seemed to be less well in 1985 than it was in 1965. A National Commission on Excellence in Education reported in 1983 that "if an unfriendly foreign power had attempted to impose on America the mediocre educational performance that exists today, we might well have viewed it as an act of war." But we allowed it to happen to ourselves. "We have, in effect, been committing an act of unthinking, unilateral educational disarmament."[50]

The commission discovered that on internationally administered achievment examinations, Americans never finished first or second and were often last. Twenty-three million Americans were functionally illiterate. High-school students were scoring lower on standardized tests than students did twenty-five years ago. Scholastic Aptitude Test (SAT) scores had declined consistently since 1963, and the number and proportion of students demonstrating superior achievement on the tests had declined. Moreover, the educational deficiencies occurred at a time when the demand for highly skilled workers was accelerating. "For the first time in the history of our country, the educational skills of one generation will not surpass, will not equal, will not even approach, those of their parents."[51]

The commission discovered the intense dedication of the American people to education and examined specific deficiencies in the programs and instruction of the schools, including the fact that one-fifth of all four-year public colleges must ac-

49. Ibid., pp. 484–90.
50. National Commission on Excellence in Education, *A Nation at Risk: The Imperative for Educational Reform* (Washington, D.C.: Government Printing Office, April, 1983), p. 5.
51. Ibid., pp. 8–9, 11.

cept a high-school graduate irrespective of grades or courses pursued. Comparisons were made with educational programs in other countries, such as England, where the average student spent 220 days per year for eight hours a day in school, compared to the American student's 180 days for six hours per day. Too many teachers in the public schools came from the bottom quarter of college graduates and were trained in "methods" rather than content. Teacher salaries were low, and one-half of the newly employed teachers of mathematics, science, and English were not qualified to teach those subjects.[52]

The commission recommended that requirements for high-school graduation be strengthened substantially to include four years of English, three years of mathematics, three years of science, three years of social studies, and one-half year of computer science. Two years of a foreign language were also recommended for those going to college. Grading standards in the high schools should be strengthened, and colleges should raise admission standards. Teaches should demonstrate an aptitude for teaching and competence in their subject field. Salaries should be increased, and a career ladder and master teacher program should be implemented.[53] There were many other recommendations, many of which have already been implemented by states and local school systems. Money is no longer the answer to education; standards and action are.

The future will bring more rigorous educational programs and standards at all levels. The emphasis will be on efficiency. We cannot and will not spend our way to academic excellence. "Knowledge, learning, information, and skilled intelligence," the commission reported, are the keys to successful world competition and survival. "Learning is the indispensable investment required for success in the 'information age' we are entering."[54]

52. Ibid., pp. 20–23.
53. Ibid., pp. 25–31.
54. Ibid., p. 7.

CHAPTER FIVE

Politics in the Postindustrial Era

What's going on? Is the American voter really becoming politically more conservative and, if so, what does that new conservatism mean? What about liberalism, particularly of the New Deal variety? Is the increasing political activism of women likely to change the style or fundamental structures of the party system? Are our parties and our people really becoming more homogenized, more alike than unlike, more in accord than in disagreement? What can we expect as the political consequences of the baby boom and the maturing and aging of those voting citizens? Even more important, what is happening in the world around us?

Moscow continues to build its military armaments, the United States prepares "star wars" defenses, and many Western countries have lowered their guard. Totalitarian regimes dominate in Africa. Democracy is on the defensive in Latin America. Americans have assumed the guilt for the world's problems and seem spiritually enervated. Is democracy likely to survive in a world seemingly bent upon its destruction?

There will be relatively little agreement on the answers to these questions. Forecasting election returns within months or weeks of an election can be hazardous at best; predicting the future of American or world politics some decades or half-century hence is probably impossible. One has only to look at the apparent great swings in political alignments of the past to imagine the difficulty of projecting future trends. Who would have imagined in 1824 that Andrew Jackson of Tennessee would be elected the president of the United States four years later, and who seriously believed even days before the election that Harry Truman would be re-elected in 1948? Who would have seriously anticipated that President Ronald Reagan might personally, and with some reasonable opportunity for success, obtain viable disarmament agreements from a Soviet premier?

Despite the kinks or shifts that personalities and traumatic events or issues can cause in the political spectrum, there is an environment in which the American political system operates. It has in the past and will likely continue to give our politics its special format. There are also some common objectives and trends shared by the world family of nations that generate certain rational possibilities. We can draw some reasonable inferences about the not too distant future of the American political system and of the world political order. At the very least, considering those things we can identify as trends will sharpen our perception of the current political environment.

Changes in the
American Political Environment

President Ronald Reagan's strong electoral victory in November, 1984, has been interpreted in a variety of ways. Democrats, liberals, and their friends in the media argue that the victory was essentially a personal one for Reagan, a likable man who had presided over four years of relative peace and prosperity. There was, such observers believe, no ideological content in the vote, and certainly no "mandate" for anything. Republicans and conservatives argue that the Reagan victory was a defeat for liberalism and a mandate for less government, more defense, and a social agenda that would allow school prayer and prohibit abortion.

Both of these analyses involve a lot of wishful thinking. Reagan's victory was, in part, a personal triumph. The American people liked and trusted the president. But national polls also suggest that the 1984 Republican victory was based on more than personality. The American people did indicate their preference for a militarily stronger America and for lower taxes and less government involvement in domestic affairs. There is, however, little evidence that the 1984 elections marked a victory for the old conservatism that Ronald Reagan once preached. Americans in 1984 were voting for a different Ronald Reagan than the one they voted for in 1980.

In 1980, Reagan promised to eliminate the Departments of Education and Energy. He pledged not to sit down with the Soviet Union in arms negotiations until Soviet troops were out of Afghanistan. He urged dramatic cuts in expensive social programs. In 1984, he did not advise any cuts in social programs, referred with some pride to government-subsidized housing for ten million people, and opposed any reduction in Social Security benefits. He also affirmed his desire for arms negotiations and agreements with the Soviet Union, which he pursued in person and at Geneva.[1] When voters cast their ballots for Ronald Reagan in 1984, were they voting for the "old conservative" or for the "new moderate"?

Reagan did not carry the Republican congressional candidates along with him. Republicans made smaller gains in the House of Representatives than they had hoped for and lost several Senate seats. President Reagan's coattails were not long enough to pull along an ideological working majority in Congress. Some polls indicate that, although voters may have preferred Ronald Reagan to Walter Mondale, they were often closer to the Democratic party than the Republican on issues. Recent voting trends do seem to indicate that the old Democratic party coalition of blacks, the South, labor, and ethnic groups is disintegrating. In addition, it would appear that the traditional liberal rhetoric of "rich man, poor man" is losing its appeal. Most Americans seem to share Ronald Reagan's caution and lack of faith in the long-term benefits of negotiating with the Soviet Union. Most seem to prefer peace through strength.

There is some evidence, according to news commentator Richard Reeves and other analysts, that the American electorate has indeed made a step toward a more conservative consensus, somewhere between the conservative rhetoric of Reagan and the old-fashioned liberalism of Mondale. Voters seemed to be for the retention, but not for the expansion, of New

---

1. Allan C. Brownfeld, "The Changing American Political Consensus," *Roll Call* (November 15, 1984): 12–22.

Deal–style welfare programs. Americans heavily prefer both a strong military defense posture and progress on arms control. The new electoral consensus has in some respects united old liberalism and old conservatism in fundamental ways.[2]

Phil Gramm, a one-time Democratic congressman and successful 1984 Republican candidate from Texas for the U.S. Senate, reflects the new consensus position. "We are not here," he says, "to repeal the New Deal. Our agenda is to cut government . . . to contain the growth of government in the belief that the private sector, the national economy, will grow over it as time goes on."[3] Another indication of the new consensus is that many of the younger voters, particularly those categorized as "young upwardly mobile professionals" ("Yuppies"), felt comfortable supporting either a liberal Democrat such as Sen. Gary Hart, or a conservative Republican such as Ronald Reagan. Everett Carll Ladd, director of the Roper Center for Public Opinion Research at the University of Connecticut, explains that politics has become more personal than partisan: "Contemporary political conflict is not so much *between social groups,* where politicians must bring together enough groups to establish a majority, as it is *within individuals,* where they must appeal to contrasting predispositions in the very same people."[4] It makes politics much more confusing and issues less clear. It means a growing homogenization of the American political order.

When asked in opinion surveys if they agreed with President Reagan that "government is not the solution to our problems; government is the problem," voters tended to straddle the fence. This could be a sign of a more sophisticated voter who realizes that government is a persistent mix of both the helpful and the harmful. Ladd believes that the new voter profile shows a mass public that is still strongly committed to expanding government, but that now is troubled by that expansion. The public, in other words, believes that things such as abortion should be a matter of individual choice, but they are deeply troubled by the social consequences deriving from such choice. Drinking is a matter of personal choice, but driv-

2. Richard Reeves, "America's Choice: What It Means," *New York Times Magazine* (November 4, 1984): 30.
3. Ibid.
4. Ibid.

ing while intoxicated is not; wearing seat belts in automobiles should be a matter of personal choice, but the social costs of not wearing seat belts are very large.[5] How one votes, then, often becomes a matter of personal choice as much as a matter of well-defined issues.

It is interesting, Richard Reeves notes, that in the same week that Sen. Walter Mondale publicly opposed new spending programs, David Stockman, then Reagan's budget director, advised that there should be no significant cuts in spending for welfare programs. Although the Reagan administration has certainly not dismantled the welfare state, it has apparently leveled off the proportion of GNP being absorbed by government at approximately 24 percent, after years of a steady rate of growth.[6]

That this new consensus may have a long life can in part be inferred from the fact that there has been a distinct shift in the voting patterns of younger Americans within recent years. An unexpected development of the 1984 presidential elections was that young voters, particularly those between eighteen and twenty-nine and most especially those between eighteen and twenty-four, indicated strong support for the re-election of President Reagan. This reversed the traditional voting pattern of college students and other young people, who have traditionally voted liberal and have supported the Democratic party.

If the baby boomers voted as a unit, or even with a predominant and consistent pattern, the significance would be enormous. These people currently compose about one-third of the total U.S. population. Traditionally, a large percentage of these seventy-five million voters would have voted Democrat, or liberal and Democrat. In the 1976 elections, 52 percent voted for Carter and 48 percent for Gerald Ford. In 1980, 45 percent of the voters within this age group voted for Jimmy Carter and 44 percent for Ronald Reagan. In 1984, 50 percent voted for Reagan and 50 percent for Mondale and the Democrats. In the past four elections, this large voter group has tended to split its vote evenly. The number of young people aged eighteen

5. Allan C. Brownfeld, "'84 Campaign's Big Surprise — Swing of Young Voters to GOP," New York City Tribune (October 20, 1984).

6. Reeves, "America's Choice," pp. 29–32, 34–35, 38.

to twenty-four who consider themselves Republicans jumped from 18 percent in 1980, to 27 percent in 1984.[7] All of these statistics suggest a distinctly conservative voting trend, which can be expected to grow as the group ages.

The economic, religious, ethnic, and regional forces that caused sharp political divisions among their parents may have little effect on the baby boom generation. It is their view of the future and their perception of the choices afforded by the political parties that determine their political decisions and inevitably shape our political future. And these voters have different perceptions of the world from their parents'. The son of the plumber and the son of the doctor are more alike than are their parents. Racial prejudice is less pronounced among the young, as evidenced in surveys by a much greater willingness to support a black for president, as well as by the growing number of blacks being elected mayors of major cities. The old ethnic differences that once characterized voting behavior are less apparent. Polls indicated, for example, that Italian-Americans strongly preferred Reagan/Bush to Mondale/Ferraro, despite Geraldine Ferraro's Italian ancestry. Party identification is not as strong as it once was, and family political traditions have less bearing. Young people are less likely to cast their first votes the way their parents vote. For a host of reasons, American society and American politics are becoming more homogeneous.[8]

In numerous polls prior to the 1984 election, President Reagan received the strongest support among people in the eighteen to twenty-four age group. Members of this group registered as Republicans rather than as Democrats or independents by ratios of two and three to one, reversing a forty-year trend to enroll as Democrats. According to Republican pollster Robert Teeter, "For the first time since Roosevelt there is a significant group in the electorate who are Republican in greater overall numbers than Democrats. If these people stay loyal, you may have a much stronger Republican Party."[9] Teeter attributes Reagan's appeal to his ideas of promoting economic growth and creating new job opportunities.

7. Brownfeld, "'84 Campaign's."
8. Ibid.
9. Ibid.

There are indicators of the conservative trend among young people in areas other than voting. Polls indicate that, whereas in 1970, 56 percent of entering college freshmen favored abolishing the death penalty, only 29 percent of that group favored ending it in 1983. Twelve percent fewer freshmen now want to legalize marijuana than did so in 1970. In 1970, 44 percent of entering freshmen preferred abolishing grading for college courses, but in 1983 only 15 percent wanted to abolish grades.[10]

The traditional view of the Democratic party as the party of reform and of the Republican party as the status quo, standpat party is also changing. Young voters are more wary of the Democratic party because they see its support for union, high wages, and protectionism as opposition to change. Although there may be some credibility to the argument that the Reagan election had more to do with style than with substance, Prof. Amitai Etzioni, a Democrat, points out that had Reagan been advocating "Zen Buddhism, unilateral disarmament and sexual license" instead of God, family, and country, his rating would have crashed. "No matter how great an actor he is, the script is still what matters to most Americans."[11]

M. Stanton Evans, a conservative author and columnist, suggests that the Reagan election victories in 1980 and 1984 are simply part of a movement that has been under way for some time and that has worldwide dimensions. In a variety of polls conducted since 1970, self-designated conservatives have consistently outnumbered self-designated liberals:

Year/Poll	% Conservative	% Liberal
1970 (Gallup)	46	28
1971 (Gallup)	45	25
1976 (Michigan)	31	17
1977 (Roper)	40	25
1979 (CBS/NYT)	34	20
1981 (Gallup)	44	20
1983 (Roper)	43	20
1984 (CBS/NYT)	35	17

Evans concludes that Reagan's election victories should hardly be a surprise, "since he has been the nation's most au-

10. Ibid.
11. Ibid.

dible spokesman for conservative causes in recent years."[12]

The conservative trend is also visible internationally. The world has been moving away from the idea of state control and state responsibility for everything.

Robert Wesson, a senior research fellow at the Hoover Institution, has remarked that, although previously it seemed most unlikely that a person of the ideological bent of Ronald Reagan could become president of the land of the New Deal, the Fair Deal and the Great Society, by 1980 it had become indeed plausible. The governments of almost all major industrial countries, including Canada, Japan, Great Britain, Germany and Italy, have become more conservative. Even the French Socialists, who came to power in 1981 with the determination and the rhetoric for nationalization of industries, have adopted policies of retrenchment and stabilization and emphasize production and profits.[13]

A more conservative trend in governmental policy is also evident in the non-Western world and in Third World countries. China, for example, has moved from the radicalism of Mao and the leftists who would abolish private property to the pragmatism of Deng, "who urges the peasants to get rich on their own, and sanctions private trade." India also has given up blueprints for socialist industrialization and is seeking foreign and domestic private investment capital. Rather than accepting the belief that the key to economic development lies in state control and planning, the contrary view is becoming more commonly accepted, that is, that open trade and decontrol are better avenues for growth.[14] In reality, the explanation for what is happening among the voting public in the United States, or within foreign governments, cannot be labeled accurately either "liberal" or "conservative."

Some of the more contemporary voting patterns are a paradox when compared to ideological structures and go beyond the liberalism and conservatism of past rhetoric. For example, in 1982, California voters approved tax-cut initiatives, re-

12. M. Stanton Evans, "It's Conservatism Two to One," *Human Events* (February 2, 1985): 7.

13. Robert Wesson, "The Conservative Political Tide Continues," *Houston Post* (November 1, 1984).

14. Ibid.; David Boaz, "Yuppies and the Future of American Politics," *Cato Policy Report* (November/December, 1984).

jected gun control, and endorsed a nuclear freeze, all of which reflected the position of no politician or political party. In Massachusetts, voters rejected attempts to weaken the Proposition 2½ tax cut, and their neighbors in Vermont were gathering in more than one hundred town meetings in support of a nuclear freeze. The Americans for Democratic Action, which has acted as the conscience of the liberal Democratic tradition, in 1982 rated Rep. William Green (R-N.Y.) and Rep. Ike Skelton (D-Mo.) at 50 percent for their congressional voting record. But the two congressmen agreed on only five of nineteen issues, with Green voting liberal on social issues and conservative on economics, and Skelton voting conservative on social issues and liberal on economic questions. Polls are showing consistent voter preference for balancing the budget and a nuclear freeze, the former generally considered a conservative program and the latter a liberal objective.[15]

If nothing else, what all this may mean is simply that the traditional liberal/conservative dichotomy no longer applies. William S. Maddox and Stuart A. Lilie argue this rather convincingly. A person's economic standing no longer predicts voting behavior. The ideological distinction between the blue-collar and white-collar worker has faded and will continue to do so as we progress into the postindustrial society. Because of broad-based improvements in educational attainment, mass media exposure for politics and social issues, and the general increase in society's affluence, the old class-based differentiation between liberal and conservative has less meaning. What the public is thinking and doing is not "politics as usual."[16]

Maddox and Lilie argue in *Beyond Liberal and Conservative* that contemporary belief systems are better understood in terms of the attitude toward government intervention on the one hand, and the attitude toward the maintenance or expansion of personal freedoms on the other. They would categorize political opinion as liberal, conservative, libertarian, and populist. Liberals, they say, support government intervention in the economy and the expansion of personal freedoms; conservatives oppose both; libertarians are for greater personal

15. Boaz, "Yuppies."
16. William S. Maddox and Stuart A. Lilie, *Beyond Liberal and Conservative* (Washington, D.C.: Cato Institute, 1984), p. 42.

freedom and oppose government intervention; and populists are for government intervention in the economy and oppose the expansion of personal freedoms.[17]

Americans have demonstrated a reluctance to describe themselves as liberal or conservative, because the terms are no longer applicable. Political scientists, pollsters, and journalists, however, have persisted in offering only those options when there are clearly, and probably always have been, more than two political perspectives in the United States.[18] Those political perspectives are much like the colors of the rainbow in that they shade into one another so that it is indeed difficult to know where a conservative, liberal, populist, or libertarian begins or ends. It is, in fact, that shading that helps make the American political system work. Hard lines, castes, and classes are difficult to identify and will be more so in the future.

Although the baby boom generation has become the "liberal cutting edge of society" on cultural and social issues, it has been moderate to conservative on economic issues. This group, however, has not had the real political impact that might have been anticipated for several reasons. Most important, it has generally remained outside of the political process. Large numbers have not become active voters or party affiliates. Those who have, have tended to divide almost equally in their political affiliation. Even those who would tend to identify themselves as liberal and Democrat are divided. For example, in the 1984 Democratic primary, Sen. Gary Hart ran to the "left and the right of Mondale at the same time." Mondale attracted the center groups of old New Dealers, populist Democrats, and traditional liberals, whereas Hart drew many of the younger voters who supported his attack on outmoded economic programs and special-interest politics.[19] Hart's following was more conservative on economic issues and liberal to libertarian on social issues.

The proportion of Americans who describe their views as "right of center" has grown since 1976, with a corresponding decline in the ranks of those who describe themselves as "left

17. Ibid., p. 4.
18. Ibid., pp. vii–xvi.
19. Ibid.

of center." In 1976, 31 percent of the respondents in a Gallup poll placed themselves to the right of center, 24 percent to the left, and 45 percent embraced the "middle." In 1984, 36 percent of the respondents placed themselves to the right, 18 percent to the left, and 46 percent in the center. George Gallup concluded that the trend toward the right reflects the growing numbers of Americans claiming affiliation with the Republican party. He noted that the proportion of voters claiming allegiance to the Democratic party was as low as it had been since the end of World War II.[20]

Other polls seem to support Gallup's analysis. A poll taken for the Republican party in November, 1984, showed that 47 percent of the adults identified with the Republicans and 41 percent with the Democrats. In a postelection survey conducted by the *New York Times* and CBS News, 47 percent of the public labeled itself Republican or independent with Republican tendencies.[21] Republican party leaders see these results as evidence of a significant political realignment.

Speaking before the U.S. Senate on May 1, 1984, Sen. Paul Tsongas (D-Mass.) said that Democrats had failed to convince the public that the Democratic party could run the economy. Democrats, he said, are viewed as people who care less about how well the economy is doing and more about "how to distribute the golden eggs. The goose's health is irrelevant." Tsongas used himself as an example to argue that the label is probably deserved:

> When I was on the House side, I remembered that the late Bill Steiger had an amendment that dealt with the capital gains tax, reducing it. I voted against it. Do you know why I voted against it? Because I was a Democrat. I considered the ethic in the House among my fellow colleagues that this was pro-business and therefore, since it is pro-business, we are against it. So I voted against it. That bill which I did not support did more for the economy of my state than anything I did as congressman.[22]

20. George Gallup, Jr., "Pull of Political Ideologies Finds a Trend to the Right," *Washington Post* (December 1, 1984).
21. "Pull Finds Republican Gains," *New York Times* (January 26, 1985).
22. Richard L. Lesher, *The Voice of Business*, newsletter (February 4, 1985).

Alan Webber, associate editor of the *Harvard Business Review*, declares that the Democratic party is like the "Chrysler Corporation of American politics." It is waiting for a Lee Iacocca to lead it back to respectability. But Webber says it will take more than a super-salesman; the Democrats need a new set of "operating principles to guide their effort to turn the party around." He believes that the Democratic party has become overly sensitive to the Washington establishment, rather than listening to the "interests and wishes of the country. Changing the Democratic Party," he says, "means getting out of Washington."[23] Democrats need a fresh infusion of ideas from outside the capital beltway.

Traditional issue-oriented, interest-oriented politics simply does not apply as it once did. The Democrats, according to Webber, have tried to match up programs with interest groups such as blue-collar workers, blacks, women, and farmers. But instead of there being a tyranny of special interests, special-interest politics has become irrelevant. For example, Gov. Mario Cuomo of New York was able to unite feminists, blacks, hardhats, and other groups behind the common appeal of a "family" theme. Members of a family can disagree on many issues, but still stand behind their shared values. Political power must be rooted in shared values and shared experiences, in the sense of community that goes beyond special-interest groups. Michigan's governor, Jim Blanchard, for example, created a common stake and a common pride in the "Michigan story" of economic comeback.[24]

Nationally, the Republican party seems to have created a community or unifying theme. Republicans have won four of the last five presidential elections and they have won an average of 82.4 percent of the electoral vote, approaching Franklin Roosevelt's four-election record of 88.3 percent of the electoral vote. Unlike the Democrats, however, the Republicans have accumulated this record with three different candidates. Columnist George Will analyzes this feat in an eloquent commentary.

23. Alan Webber, "What the Democrats Must Do to Recover," *New York Times* (January 28, 1985).

24. George Will, "Realignment Is a Fact," *Washington Post* (November 7, 1984).

Will believes that the 1984 elections "buried the most ideologically uniform and liberal ticket in American history." It was, he said, a quixotic offering to an electorate that was more conservative than at any time since 1952. The results were not the result of a fluke, or of weak Democratic candidates, or of the Reagan charm and personality. In the past four elections, Will noted, the Democrats tried to sell the voting public McGovern, Carter twice, and Mondale. The election results were not aberrations; on the contrary, they were caused by the Democratic party's ignoring the public's attitudes on issues.[25] Reagan has demonstrated that in a democracy you build a political base by saying a few things clearly and convincingly over and over again.

There is a growing body of informed opinion that believes that the social programs adopted by the Democrats during the 1960s failed to solve social problems, even exacerbated them. In his widely discussed book, *Losing Ground,* Charles Murray, senior research fellow at the Manhattan Institute for Policy Research, shows that the great proliferation of social programs in the mid-sixties made it profitable for the poor to behave in the short term in ways that were destructive in the long term. That is, the dramatic increase in illegitimate births, single-parent families, and dropouts from the work force was a perfectly rational response to such programs as Aid to Families with Dependent Children.

Under welfare rules in 1960, the incentive was for couples to marry, have children, and go to work (not necessarily in that order.) Under the new regulations, a female welfare recipient with a child can draw fifty dollars per week in cash and eleven dollars in food stamps, receive rent subsidies of varying value, and have medical insurance under Medicaid. The minimum welfare package adds up to twenty-three dollars more than the purchasing power of forty hours of work at a minimum wage job. Moreover, the rules allow for supplemental income from working. A couple is financially better off if the father does not work at a minimum wage job. Furthermore, marriage offers no financial advantage to either partner, but, on the contrary, results in the loss of the federal aid

25. Ibid.

for the dependent children. Moreover, there is incentive in the system to have more illegitimate children.[26]

Massive illegitimacy in the black community, Charles Murray believes, may be a rational response to the destructive incentives that social programs have created. But the incentives are equally as strong for both the white and the black family to "drop out." Because of the disincentives created by welfare programs, Republican party spokespersons believe that the collapse of the welfare state as an intellectual concept has contributed to the fact that the Republican party is on the threshold of political dominance. Congressman Newt Gingrich (R-Ga.) believes that four factors have converged to enhance Republican popularity: a shift in power nationally to traditionally more conservative regions; the rise of the modern conservative movement; the collapse of the welfare state as a viable alternative; and Ronald Reagan's personal ability to communicate.[27]

Republican Jack Kemp (R-N.Y.) says that President Reagan's "quarterbacking, his leadership, his ability to motivate" have been instrumental in recent successes of the Republican party, but he believes these traits capitalize on "some good resources" to move the party to potential majority status. Peter D. Hart, Walter Mondale's pollster, thinks that one of the major Republican "resources" was the breakdown among Democrats. There was no "awful miscalculation" in 1983 that led to the defeats of 1984, he said; "the erosion has been there for 16 years."[28] Sen. Gary Hart, whose unsuccessful campaign in 1984 helped expose the Democratic party's problems, attributes Republican success less to Reagan than to the party's being able to capitalize on the period of transition within the Democratic party. He says that the party has run out of steam in terms of themes, substance, and ideas. A vacuum has formed and Reagan has been able to fill it partly. But the real question, he says, is what happens after Reagan.[29]

Democratic pollster Patrick Caddell says that since 1978 the

26. George Murray, *Losing Ground* (New York: Basic Books, 1984), pp. 160–61.

27. Ibid.; Dan Balz, "GOP Sees Itself on Threshold of Political Dominance," *Washington Post* (January 21, 1984).

28. Balz, "GOP Sees Itself on Threshold."

29. Ibid.

Democratic party has been the party of the status quo, whereas the Republicans have embraced supply-side economics and become the vehicle for a new surge of intellectual energy.[30] The Republicans have gained a big plus by identifying inflation as public enemy number one and then apparently defeating that enemy. The next objective is to combat the deficit, which most Americans now identify as being of primary importance. The key to this will be to control government spending and to facilitate, or at least to hope for, some continued growth in the economy. If these things can occur, some Republicans believe that their party could achieve a political majority for the rest of the twentieth century.[31] One of the interesting things about domestic political trends is that there are echos or reflections of these developments in the Western world, major industrial nations of the East, and even in communist nations.

Political Trends in Other Nations

Freedom is a nebulous thing, and more precious than most Americans realize. Freedom House, a respected human rights organization based in New York City, reports that in 1985 two billion people, that is, two of every five, lived in fifty-five countries that were "not free." About one-fourth of the world's people live in countries that are defined as "partly free," and one-third live in "free" countries. There have, however, been substantial changes under way, with particularly impressive gains in the Americas. Freedom House notes that Argentina has returned to democratic rule and that every Central American country has improved its "freedom" rating. Uruguay held its first free election in years, and Brazil followed. Paraguay, Chile, Barbados, and the Dominican Republic became less free.[32]

Freedom House also concludes that African freedoms deteriorated markedly in 1985. Nigeria accepted a military regime. Sudan, Ghana, Kenya, Liberia, Burkina Faso, and Cameroon curtailed individual liberties. Most increased press

---

30. Ibid.
31. Ibid.
32. *Freedom Monitor* (New York: Freedom House, January, 1985), p. 4.

censorship. South Africa has now virtually precluded access by the free international press. Africa is not alone. Seventy-five percent of the nations of the world practice some degree of print and electronic media control or supervision.[33]

Although much of Africa remains under the control of one-party authoritarian regimes, the trends in other parts of the world indicate an expansion of personal liberties and freedom. Whereas in 1979, only two South American nations, Colombia and Venezuela, had democratic governments, today eight of the twelve are democracies or military regimes preparing to convert to democratic government. Although reporter Timothy O'Leary has described elections in some countries, such as Brazil and Uruguay, as less than perfect, they are nonetheless a strong transitional step to democracy. Ecuador was the first to move to a democratic government in 1979. Peru followed, and in 1982, Hernán Siles Zuazo was elected president of Bolivia, ending eighteen years of military rule there. Argentina ended seven years of military rule in 1983 with the election of Raúl Alfonsín.[34]

These developments have occurred in contradiction to the traditional view that democracy flourishes best under healthy economic conditions. South American nations generally are heavily indebted, and inflation is rampant. Brazil has the largest foreign debt — over one hundred billion dollars — and a 224 percent annual inflation rate. Bolivia has suspended payments on its eighteen billion dollar debt and has a 100 percent inflation rate. Argentina owes forty-five billion dollars and has a 700 percent inflation rate.[35] Democratization has come in the face of some difficult economic times, which makes the phenomenon even more remarkable.

The *Washington Post* viewed the election of a civilian president in Brazil in 1985 as a singularly important step toward democratization in South America. "The passage from authoritarian government to democracy is always difficult," the editor wrote. In the Brazilian case, the generals clearly intended to steer the election to a civilian member of their own party, but they had removed most of the constraints on speech,

33. Timothy O'Leary, "Military Regimes Losing Grip in Latin America," *Washington Times* (January 21, 1985).
34. Ibid.
35. "Brazil Elects a President," *Washington Post* (January 16, 1985).

the press, and assembly. During the elections it became clear that most of the voters preferred an opposition candidate, and the generals abided by that choice without interfering in the course of the election but knowing the outcome. "With the election of Mr. Neves, Brazil greatly strengthens the trend toward democracy throughout South America," the *Post* editorialized.[36]

For a time there was evidence that important changes toward a more free and open society in South Africa were occurring. In November, 1983, voters endorsed a new constitution that brought Indians and members of the colored (mixed race) group into the political process for the first time. Although this reform failed to achieve the goals of blacks, it represented a moderation of the apartheid system and a move in the direction of a multiracial society. Alan Paton, author of *Cry the Beloved Country*, a classic novel about race relations in South Africa, sees progress despite the violence and the dangerous course the government is pursuing. "Those people who expect our politicians to get off the tiger immediately and say, 'I love you, tiger, . . .' are asking for the moon." But the government is attempting the impossible by making a constitution that will get South Africa "off the tiger."[37]

There have been signs of the weakening of apartheid. Stellenbosch University, the leading Afrikaans-language university, now enrolls nonwhite students in graduate and undergraduate courses that are not offered at one of the three black universities. The *Christian Science Monitor* viewed the admission of nonwhites to this bastion of racial exclusivity as a complete reversal of National party apartheid policy.[38] Before the Stellenbosch decision, the English-language universities of Cape Town and Witwatersrand were each permitting about five hundred black students to attend. Some of the bits of "pretty" apartheid were being dismantled. Black unions were flourishing, and urban blacks were being considered for constitutional recognition. Wages for blacks tripled between 1970 and 1979, and the wage gap between whites and blacks has narrowed in all sectors. In 1970, whites earned twenty times

36. Ibid.
37. Allan C. Brownfeld, "South Africa's Importance to the Free World," *America's Future* (1984).
38. Ibid.

the salary of blacks; in 1979, the disparity had fallen to seven times as much as blacks.[39]

In 1979, the South African government amended the labor laws to remove job reservations and to open trade union membership to "all workers irrespective of race." South African law now guarantees all workers the right to work, to organize, and to join employee organizations, as well as the right to bargain collectively. All laborers are entitled to fair remuneration, equitable conditions of service, access to training and retraining, safety and health in the workplace, unemployment insurance and workmen's compensation, and protection against unfair labor practices.[40] By the end of 1985, however, racial progress and reform seemed to have come to an end, as violence and police repression mounted.

World opinion and pressure have come out against apartheid. The nation appears to be poised on a precipice, one side of which will bring dramatic racial and social reform and the other a retreat into a violent, repressive, and reclusive society. The optimists, however, see the constitution of 1983 as a new beginning and the strong economic health of South Africa as a tremendous incentive to solve the admittedly difficult problems of racial and tribal hostility. There is every reason to be hopeful about the direction of South Africa's internal politics.

For the most part, there has been a definite trend among nations of the world to a greater concern for and protection of human rights and personal freedom. The strong advocacy of the United States has contributed to this trend. There has also been, in many diverse and unexpected places, a movement toward limited government and a free market.

Observations on the Economic Health of Nations

In Western Europe there has been a turning away from the welfare state and centralized government and a movement in the direction of limited government and a free market. This

39. Richard E. Sincere, Jr., *The Politics of Sentiment* (Washington, D.C.: Ethics and Public Policy Center, 1984), p. 77.
40. Ibid., p. 82; Brownfeld, "South Africa's Importance."

reverses the trend since World War II. Asia, the Third World countries, and even communist nations have demonstrated a loosening of economic controls and tolerance, if not support for free-market operations and private enterprise.

Britain's Conservative leader, Margaret Thatcher, the nation's longest continuously serving prime minister, has reduced the degree to which government can be called to solve economic problems. She has eliminated many market controls, such as those on overseas investment, wages, and prices; she has confronted directly the power of labor unions; and she has sold about eight billion dollars' worth of state-owned industries.[41] Thatcher's government has also succeeded in reducing inflation from 20 percent to 5 percent.

Prof. David Butler of Oxford University says that under her leadership the "complex of British life has changed." She is "among the small group of leaders who are able to articulate hopes and fears, and they change hearts and minds and shift political opinion. I think Mrs. Thatcher detected, after 30 years basically of the welfare state, a growing disillusion with bureaucracy, a feeling that people had to pay too much in tax, and she very skillfully turned that against socialism."[42] Peter Jenkins, a political opponent and columnist for The Guardian, agrees that "her government has brought the country face to face with its decline and administered a shock to the system, which has been most salutary and overdue."[43]

In France, President François Mitterrand, a socialist, found that the traditional socialist policies were leading France toward financial collapse. He reversed the expansionist policies of 1981, and adopted measures bringing about deflation. His 1985 budget provided for reduced taxes and lower governmental spending, echoing the "supply-side" economics of the Reagan administration. Mitterrand sought to hold deficit spending to 3 percent of the total budget and required nationalized firms to operate at a profit.[44] His conservative fiscal policies have led to an end of the "union of the Left" with the French Communist party.

41. Michael Getler, "After 10 Years as Tory Leader, Thatcher in Control," Washington Post (February 10, 1985).
42. Ibid.
43. Ibid.
44. "Boxed in Mitterrand," The Economist (January 28, 1985).

At the Communist party's twenty-fifth Congress in Paris in February, 1985, party leader George Marchais declared an end to a twenty-five-year-old political strategy of attempting to reach power by forming a union with the Socialists. He accused the Socialist government of failing to implement a joint program agreed on with the Communists following a left-wing election victory in May, 1981. Marchais charged that the Socialists "posed as the guarantors of the union of the left in order to divide and demobilize the working-class movement and reduce the influence of the Communist Party."[45] The political reality is that the French Communist party now receives only 10 percent of the vote, compared to the 20 to 28 percent received in the decades following World War II. This reflects substantive changes in French life and the rise in standards of living and education which work against an authoritarian Marxist party with a fixed view of the world.[46]

Throughout Western Europe welfare costs are rising at an alarming rate. Countries that were paying an average of 19.3 percent of GNP into social programs in 1970 are now devoting about one-third of their funds to welfare. Governments are now trying to cut back on social spending. In France, the socialist regime of François Mitterrand curtailed its far-reaching spending plans. In Denmark, once considered a model of welfare state success, Prime Minister Paul Schluter has called for "privatizing" industries and pension schemes. In Britain and in West Germany (which spends $4.8 billion a month on retirement benefits) there has been talk about limiting the benefits now available to all citizens and turning the welfare state into a "safety net" that would assist only the "truly needy."[47]

Western Europe's high unemployment has placed great strain on the welfare systems. Unemployed in Britain may receive benefits greater than their salaries. Holland cut all social benefits, including unemployment payments, by 10 to 15

45. Michael Dobbs, "French Communist Leader Marchais Drops 'Union of the Left,'" *Washington Post* (February 9, 1985).

46. Flora Lewis, "France's Fading Reds," *New York Times* (February 4, 1985); "What's on the Left," *Washington Post* (February 9, 1985).

47. *Freedom and Economics: A World-Wide Survey of Economic Freedoms Existing Today* (Houston: Citizens Economic Foundation, 1984), pp. 21–22.

percent in May, 1983. In June, 1983, the West German government took similar steps. Denmark now limits unemployment benefits to $200 a month for young people living alone, although the Danish Social Workers Union estimates that $275 is the absolute minimum for social necessities. Not only are governments running out of money, but many of the welfare programs have proved to be counterproductive. Europeans are responding, much as are Americans, by fiscal and political conservatism.[48]

The tiny nation of Iceland provides a microcosm of what is happening elsewhere. Iceland, a nation of only 230,000, leads the world in literacy, with a 100 percent literacy rate. The country publishes more books per capita than any other nation in the world. It has the second-highest number of automobiles per capita, led only by the United States. It is also an "advanced" welfare state on the verge of bankruptcy. The new conservative government is attempting to change directions. It is reducing or eliminating payments to students to remain in school in the free universities. The government has imposed strict controls over domestic credit and prices, and it is attempting to stabilize the exchange rate of the Icelandic krona and slow the almost 100 percent inflation rate. The intellectual and political establishment, which has championed the cradle-to-the-grave welfare system, is being challenged by a vigorous, young, pro–free market conservative group.[49]

On May 8, 1979, this group formed the Freedom Association of Iceland. One of its leaders is Hannes Gissurarson, a young history teacher who is now studying for his doctorate at Oxford University. He points out that "the nineteen seventies were years of growing government intervention in the economy and stagflation. It became obvious that the state could not solve all the problems it had taken upon itself to solve."[50] Since its founding, the Freedom Association has sponsored seminars by economists such as David Friedman, the son of Milton Friedman, who compared the Icelandic Commonwealth of A.D. 930 to A.D. 1262 to a free-market trading

48. Ibid.
49. Ibid., p. 30.
50. Ibid., pp. 23–24.

alliance. Nobel laureate Friedrich A. Hayek lectured on principles of monetary policy in 1980. Gissurarson regards these activities as part of the intellectual counterrevolution against socialism.[51]

Sweden, which also has a matured welfare state, has begun to adopt elements of a free-market economy. Sweden's experience has been that the more government spends, the less people work. The government increased its spending from 24 percent of GNP in 1950, to 64 percent in 1980, one of the highest spending records of any government in the free, industrialized world. Compared to 1960, Swedes are working 24 percent fewer hours and absenteeism is up 63 percent. Inasmuch as government takes and spends most of what the worker earns, the people are choosing to earn less.[52]

Sweden's Roine Carlsson, cabinet minister in charge of state-owned companies and a former union official, surprised financial markets in December, 1983, by selling the government-owned consumer electronics manufacturing firm, Luxor AB, for $19.5 million to Oy Nokia of Finland, a private company. The government has sold a total of $193 million in state-owned assets in sectors ranging from commercial banking to forestry to shipbuilding and it has instructed its state-owned firms to act more like private businesses, with a strong emphasis on profits.[53] Swedish trade minister Staffan Burenstam Linder says that the changes are small in terms of values, but very great when compared to the socialist dogma that has been prevalent in Swedish politics.[54]

In the Third World, the difference between those countries that have embraced socialism and those that have followed a free-market path is clear. Although population explosions have contributed to a net decline in the standard of living of nearly all African states, the decline has been most pronounced in those countries espousing socialism. Africa is the only part of the world that now grows less food for each person than it did in 1960. In nine African countries, food production per capita is 90 percent of the levels achieved in 1960. The World Bank estimates that nearly two hundred million people in

51. Ibid.
52. Ibid.
53. Ibid.
54. Ibid.

Africa, or 60 percent of the population, consume fewer calories than are required for survival.[55]

Ghana has perhaps suffered most under totalitarian socialist regimes. Since the revolution in 1957, it has had five military coups and three civilian governments. Kwame Nkrumah, the acknowledged father of African nationalism, determined to make Ghana economically independent by manufacturing all of those things previously imported. State-owned factories were soon producing cotton goods, clothing, canned foods, and rolled steel. He effectively cut Ghana off from the international economy, and Ghana produced less and less that was of interest to the outside world. In 1962, it nationalized the tobacco and cocoa plantations, and production has since steadily declined. A tax on cocoa, Ghana's major export crop, discouraged foreign sales, as did the overvalued state-mandated exchange rate for Ghanian currency.[56] As a result, Ghana has lost its sources of income and is producing costly consumer goods that could be obtained more cheaply from foreign imports.

In contrast, the Ivory Coast, with an economic base similar to Ghana's, has expanded its cocoa exports, developed new primary export products, and generally pursued free-market policies. Between 1960 and 1978, per capita income in Ghana fell from $430 to $390; in the Ivory Coast, per capita incomes rose from $540 to $940 in the same period (based on 1978 prices).[57] Generally, those states that have followed free-market policies have improved their standard of living, whereas those that have followed socialist and protectionist economic policies have fallen behind.

Those states that have made singular progress include Taiwan, Singapore, Hong Kong, and South Korea, all of which have embraced free-market policies. Ghana, India, Tanzania, Cuba, and Pakistan have followed socialist patterns. "There is not a single case," states Prof. Melvin Krauss, "where a left-wing authoritarian regime produced anything but economic dislocation, ruin and stagnation. Cuba, China, India, Tanzania, Jamaica are all economic busts . . . the biggest obstacle to the

55. Lee Griggs, "Socialism: Trials and Errors" *Time* (March 13, 1978): 24–41.
56. Melvin Krauss, *Development without Aid* (New York: McGraw-Hill, 1983), p. 30.
57. Ibid.

economic development of the Third World is big government."[58] Over the past sixteen years, the "Burmese way to socialism" has led that country from prosperity to poverty.[59] In contrast, Hong Kong is the casebook example of a free-market economy.

Milton and Rose Friedman, in their popular book *Free to Choose*, point out that Hong Kong, with 4.5 million people, four hundred square miles of territory, and a population density 185 times that of the United States, enjoys one of the highest standards of living in all of Asia, exceeded only by Japan. Hong Kong has no tariffs or other restraints on trade. Residents may buy from or sell to whom they wish. Taxes are low. There are no minimum wage laws, and no price fixing. Government spending is at the lowest per capita level in the world. "Businessmen," the Friedmans say, "can reap the benefits of their success but also bear the cost of their mistakes."[60] Economic failure seems to have become a way of life in the communist world. In many of these countries, including the Soviet Union and China, there have been major departures from traditional Marxist doctrine.

In the People's Republic of China, the current leadership has acknowledged the failure of previous economic policies. In its far-reaching effort to overhaul the economy, the government no longer assigns all workers to government jobs at fixed pay and under orders to fill production quotas set by central planners. It is encouraging a degree of free enterprise by offering tax exemptions and low-interest loans to the self-employed. Of the forty million Chinese entering the job market each year, it is estimated that more than two million will end up working for themselves or for privately financed groups.[61]

State-owned companies are now required to generate profits. In addition each is now required to pay the government a part of its profits, corresponding roughly to the corporate tax rate in the United States. The remainder of the profits are to be used for wages, plant expansion, or other purposes determined by the management of the unit, not by central plan-

58. Ibid., p. 53.
59. Griggs, "Socialism."
60. Milton Friedman and Rose Friedman, *Free to Choose* (New York: Harcourt Brace Jovanovich, 1980), p. 34.
61. *Freedom and Economics*, p. 26.

ners. In 1979, Deng Xiaoping decided to make Sichuan province the testing ground for dismantling earlier economic policies and loosening central planning. Zhao Ziyang, the Sichuan province chief, who later became prime minister, felt that "state control is too tight. Our idea is to combine the planned economy with market forces." Firms were given decision-making authority in production and marketing matters, and many factories were reorganized as "shareholders" in larger enterprises.[62] Free markets began to flourish in the province.

At first, industrial enterprises that fulfilled their annual goals were allowed to keep 5 percent of their planned profits and 20 percent of anything earned above the plan. Subsequently, all profits were to be retained by the firm, which paid an assortment of taxes to the state. The result has been an 80 percent increase in profit by the state-owned firms.[63]

There has been an even more dramatic change in China's agricultural economy. As recently as 1977, private plots for farmers in China were considered "capitalist tails that had to be cut off." In 1982, Sichuan confirmed that 15 percent of state farmland could be distributed as private plots, and farmers were allowed to diversify crops and branch out into livestock raising and cottage industries. As a result, rural savings have risen 80 percent and retail sales of television sets and radios have increased by 150 percent.[64] *Time* correspondent Richard Bernstein reported from Peking that formerly "all Chinese peasants were grouped into production teams that worked the land in common. Each laborer earned work points, which were exchanged for a ration of grain and a small cash stipend." The work points have now been abolished; each peasant is allocated a "free" parcel of land to work as he or she sees fit, and each may keep produce above a minimum quota that must be turned over to the state.[65] The result has been a better standard of living and the proliferation of free markets across China.

Chairman Deng has reaffirmed his commitment to modernizing China's economy and to opening the country to trade and commerce with the West. He "accelerated economic change by opening 14 of China's coastal cities to foreign in-

62. Ibid., pp. 26, 37–38.
63. Ibid., pp. 37–38.
64. Ibid.
65. Ibid.

vestment." He is also abolishing state purchasing quotas for grain, which have encouraged overproduction, and his successful negotiations with Great Britain to regain control of Hong Kong have effectively introduced a "one country, two system" concept. The official *People's Daily* declared that "we cannot depend on the works of Marx and Lenin to solve all of today's problems. . . . The economy is a vast sea, and there are many questions that are not written in books" to which new solutions may be required.[66]

The American press sees these developments as a bold departure on the road to free-market principles. "Personal initiative," declared *U.S. News and World Report*, "stultified by decades of official hostility, is reigniting like a prairie fire across the length and breadth of this huge country: Government tour guides today bus foreigners to visit 'rich peasants' with incomes as high as $10,000 a year. Newly organized farm teams are acquiring small airplanes for crop dusting. Farmers are being permitted to build spacious homes of their own."[67] In effect, "Peking is starting to redefine Marxism so that it can move toward the mixed market economy and the incentive system it has now chosen, without abandoning the faith."[68]

Hungary is another communist country that has been a center of economic innovation. It has the highest standard of living of any Eastern European country. It is the consumer goods center for much of the Eastern bloc. Forty percent of its agricultural production is accounted for by private farming. State-owned business may now be acquired by private firms or persons through public bids on a long-term lease basis during which period the operator receives an agreed-on percentage of the profits. Most prices are now determined by the free market, and state-owned firms are selling bonds to private investors to raise capital expansion. It is anticipated that as many as four hundred thousand workers in state-operated business may make the transition into the private economic sector that is developing.[69]

In Cuba, Fidel Castro's government has begun to move away

66. Burton Yale Pines in *Newsweek* (January 14, 1985).
67. *U.S. News and World Report* (February 4, 1985): 36.
68. Flora Lewis, "The Red Reformation," *New York Times* (January 22, 1985).
69. *U.S. News and World Report* (February 4, 1985): 43.

from the central planning and total economic control that were instituted in 1959. Factory managers are being given room for more independent judgment and initiative. A new law allows Cubans to own their own homes. Supermarkets are opening that sell scarce consumer goods at high prices, but that provide incentives for workers to increase their output. Foreign investment and tourism are being encouraged.[70]

Even in the Soviet Union, free-market incentives are being considered. Factory managers are being given a freer hand in determining production quotas and market distribution policies. Unofficially, a free market has developed on the peasant farm plots and among the carpenters, mechanics, plumbers, tailors, and other artisans in the cities.[71] According to Zurich's *Neue Zurcher Zeitung,* "the Stalinist model of a command economy is no longer able to provide the necessary production and services." Marxism-Leninism does not work in a modern industrial society, and it has proved incapable of adapting to the scientific-technical revolution that is in progress.[72] As a result, many communist nations are being forced to seek their own way, including adaptations of capitalism, and to interpret or adapt the communist ideology as best they can. Because of this, there is greater economic diversity within the Communist system than there has ever been.[73]

Crop failures and famine have sometimes been as much due to a failure of the system as to weather or natural disaster. Former U.S. ambassador to the United Nations Jeane Kirkpatrick believes that food shortages in Africa have been caused as much by socialist ideology as by drought. "Coercion has failed where market incentives might well have succeeded."[74] In Ethiopia, where starvation and hunger are among the most horrible the world has known, the government has turned an act of God into a calamity. The government of Colonel Mengistu Haile Mariam had forbidden the storage of food from earlier harvests as "hoarding." Saving money from the sale of crops was prohibited as an act of "capitalist accumulation." Earning

70. Ibid.
71. Ibid.
72. "Interview," *U.S. News and World Report* (February 4, 1985): 43.
73. Ibid.
74. Allan C. Brownfeld, "The Unreported Cause of African Starvation Is Marxist Ideology," *New York City Tribune* (November 28, 1984).

a living from transporting crops and food was labeled "exploitation." All of these acts were punishable by official extortion, or worse.[75]

Socialism has experienced its worst failures in the agricultural sector. Rural socialism and agrarian collectivism have been demonstrated failures in Europe, Asia, and Africa. Most countries are abandoning collectivized farming and adopting private farm programs, mixed production, or locally managed cooperative farms. Socialist agricultural policies eliminated the incentives for farmers to be productive. In addition, in most nations, including in Africa, the farm population has become a distinct political minority. Governments have tended to favor low food and farm prices to provide inexpensive food and fibers for urban dwellers. Low prices create a disincentive to continued market production. The more controlled the markets, as they are in socialist countries, the lower farm prices are likely to be relative to nonfarm prices, and the less efficient will be farm production.[76]

What is happening in the world around us is in some respects a reflection of what is happening here in the United States. Nations are turning away from a controlled economy and are adopting elements of the free-market system. The United States, under the Reagan administration, is stressing decontrol, reduced federal spending, and a balanced budget. The government of François Mitterrand has adopted austerity programs and requires profits of its state-owned industries. Under Margaret Thatcher, England has turned many of its state-owned manufacturing operations over to private investors and has eliminated many market controls. China has attempted to mix elements of petty capitalism with its state-coordinated economy. Sweden is reducing the level of government spending in the national economy. There seems to be a general trend among nations of the world, as there is in the United States, to get back to the basics.

Back to the Basics

This does not mean that the threat to capitalism and to democracy has diminished. The challenge posed to the free world

75. Ibid.
76. Ibid.

by the Soviet Union and its allies remains formidable. The Soviet Union continues to expand its military capability, the United States builds its star wars defenses, and the Western nations have lowered their defense and military priorities. Although socialist and communist nations may be adopting elements of capitalism, there is an inherent conflict of interests. Throughout history political liberty has existed only in societies which retained a free, or mostly free economic system where property is private and "normal economic activity consists of commercial transactions between consenting adults."[77]

Jean-François Revel, a distinguished French political commentator, believes that democracy may be something of a historical accident which for a brief moment combines the elements of a free economy and a free society. It is a political form that is by its very nature fragile and which is always vulnerable to the hosts of outside interests seemingly bent on its destruction. Totalitarian regimes do not tolerate criticism and change, but democracy requires self-criticism. That is both one of its great strengths and its weaknesses. The American people for example, have turned self-criticism into self-condemnation, and have assumed a burden of guilt. It has become "a civilization that feels guilty for everything it is and does," which drains its energies and enervates the people making them less willing to defend themselves when their existence is threatened.[78] There is evidence, however, that this naivete of the Americans and their Western allies is being replaced by a greater realism, just as the dogmatism of the Marxist-Leninist world is accepting a more realistic view of the world order.

Sir Patrick Wall, a member of the British Parliament and a specialist on strategic matters, believes that the West's current leaders are committed to unity and strength. President Reagan, Prime Minister Thatcher, President Mitterrand of France, and West Germany's Chancellor Kohl know each other, respect each other, and have demonstrated that they can work together. Wall believes that their greatest task will be to consult and act together to deal with problems before they be-

<hr />

77. Irving Kristol, "Capitalism, Socialism and Democracy," *Commentary* (April, 1978): 53–54.
78. Jean-François Revel, *Commentary* (June, 1984): 19–28.

come magnified by the media. In addition, despite ideological and other differences between the Warsaw Pact nations and the West, they do share certain common goals and values. All nations want to improve their economies and raise the standard of living. No government wants to see the world destroyed by nuclear war. Most nations genuinely want peace. Western nations particularly want to reduce unemployment and improve their technological progress. Most governments believe that these objectives can be reached at least in part by containing the arms race. It must be made clear to world leaders, Wall contends, that aggression cannot be tolerated and that those who attack cannot win.[79] There are basic values and objectives upon which world peace and a new prosperity can be built.

It is unlikely that the American people will soon come to trust the Soviet Union, but it is possible that the recognition of shared human interests can impel leaders such a Mikhail S. Gorbachev and Ronald Reagan to make real reductions in expenditures for armaments, especially when both oversee military capacities that can destroy not only the other but also much of the world. In politics, social areas, religious practices, education, and in economics, the United States and much of the world seem to be headed toward a period of preoccupation with the basics. In American society the family is likely to regain its integrity, educators will extol the virtues of the three R's, Christian religious leaders will discuss the Bible instead of political and social issues, and economists will use the rhetoric and many of the practices of supply-side economics.[80] And what will be happening in the world of the military and national defense? That will be a crucial consideration affecting the prosperity and very survival of the United States, and of the entire family of nations.

79. Patrick Wall, "Unfinished Business," *Sea Power* (February, 1985).
80. Burton Yale Pines, *Back to Basics* (New York: William Morrow and Co., 1982), pp. 267, 310; Kristol, "Capitalism, Socialism and Democracy," pp. 53–54.

CHAPTER SIX

The Future of Warfare

The dimensions of war or potential war have changed so enormously since the end of World War II that it is difficult for the layperson or even the "professional" to comprehend the technology, that is, how wars might be fought, or what the effect of future wars might be on human existence. Science fiction writers and film producers have given us sometimes lurid and certainly dramatic portrayals of "star wars" and post-nuclear holocaust possibilities. Since the close of World War II, when the United States exploded nuclear bombs over Hiroshima and Nagasaki, nuclear warfare and the threat of nuclear warfare have dominated the public's perception of modern war.

A major thrust of military development has involved the technology of nuclear weapons—atomic, hydrogen, and neutron—and systems for the delivery of and defense against such weapons. The arms race between the Soviet Union and the United States seems to have achieved a degree of world peace based on the doctrine of "mutually assured destruction" (MAD). The hazards of nuclear retaliation are so great to the initial user of such weapons that there is a deterrent force at work to discourage (but not prevent) nuclear war.

Mutually assured destruction may also have discouraged a confrontation between the superpowers with conventional weapons, on the grounds that such a confrontation might lead to the employment of nuclear weapons by one or the other. MAD has obviously not prevented conventional warfare. In fact, it could be responsible for the apparent proliferation of "subliminal warfare," such as guerrilla warfare and terrorism.

There has been almost constant nonnuclear warfare since the end of World War II. The Korean and the Vietnam wars involved massive military commitments by the United States for almost two decades. Armed conflict has been a regular part of the life-style of many people over the past half century, as indeed for most of human history. Peace has been the exception and war has been the rule for much of Latin America, Africa, the Middle East, and Southeast Asia. Direct armed conflict between the nuclear powers, primarily the United States and the Soviet Union, was a very real possibility on a number of occasions during the Korean War, in Cuba, and in the Middle East. Although the world is no longer the domain of two superpowers, the political and military realities of a Soviet bloc and a Western alliance are still very much with us and will continue to shape military responses in the foreseeable future.

NATO and the Warsaw Pact

The two major military alliances at work in the world today were constructed to defend the Western nations and the Soviet bloc nations from each other. The North Atlantic Treaty Organization (NATO) was organized in 1949, as a "response to the aggressive and expansionist foreign policy of the Soviet Union."[1] Although the United States has achieved a degree of military supremacy by virtue of its atomic weapons, by 1949 that technological advantage had eroded with the explosion of nuclear devices by the Soviet Union. Moreover, the United States' great strength in conventional weapons and land forces had evaporated rapidly after the close of World War II. By the end of 1948, the United States was returning troops to Europe to bolster the depleted armies as the reality of war between the Soviet Union and the Western allies began to seem very possible. NATO was formed to deter the threat presented by the Soviet Union and its Eastern European–bloc nations to Western Europe. The superiority of conventional Soviet and Eastern European forces was further compounded by the So-

---

1. Dennis Bark, ed., *To Promote Peace* (Stanford, Calif.: Hoover Institution Press, 1984), p. 219.

viet development of nuclear power and the dissolution of stability in Asia caused by the Chinese Communist revolution and the ouster of Chiang Kai-shek. NATO attempted to combine the military strength of the West in a front against real and imagined threats from the Soviet bloc.

NATO is now a military alliance of fifteen nations: Belgium, Britain, Canada, Denmark, France, West Germany, Greece, Italy, Luxembourg, the Netherlands, Norway, Portugal, Turkey, the United States, and Spain. It has for nearly forty years served as an effective deterrent to military aggression in Europe. As Henry Kissinger, former secretary of state, said before the 1979 NATO Conference in Brussels, "NATO, by all standards of traditional alliances, has been an enormous success. To maintain an alliance in peacetime without conflict for a generation is extremely rare in history."[2]

The military power of the NATO alliance was strengthened throughout the 1950s and part of the 1960s by U.S. possession of nuclear weapons and by the superior air power of the Western alliance. Nuclear weapons had become standard fare for science fiction writers such as H. G. Wells early in the twentieth century. Although most research was done in Europe before World War II, atomic physics was developed in the United States as well. An article published in Europe in 1938 by Otto Hahn and Lisa Meitner induced the British to begin work on a bomb, code named Tube Alloys. President Franklin D. Roosevelt authorized a small research program in 1939, after Leo Szilard urged Albert Einstein to write to FDR about the weapons' potential. Concerned about Nazi work on atomic weapons, Roosevelt urged Canada and Great Britain to cooperate with the United States in atomic research, and in 1942 the Manhattan Project was created. J. Robert Oppenheimer of Princeton's Institute for Advanced Study and Gen. Leslie Groves of the Corps of Engineers led the project to a successful atomic test in New Mexico in July, 1945. Fearing the cost of one million casualties in the projected invasion of the Japanese mainland, the United States consulted with its allies and on August 6, 1945, dropped an atomic bomb on Hiroshima. More than one hundred thousand died, and on August 9, an-

2. Kenneth Myers, ed., *NATO: The Next Thirty Years* (Boulder, Colo.: Westview Press, 1980), p. 4.

other bomb destroyed Nagasaki and killed fifty thousand more. The atomic age began in a holocaust of destruction.

As America disbanded its armies following World War II, many hoped that the newly organized United Nations and the existence of nuclear weapons would make war obsolete. U.S. attempts to impose international controls on nuclear weapons were blocked when the Soviet Union rejected on-site inspection in 1948. Within a short time, the United States had adopted a policy of "containment" and had assisted in the organization of the North Atlantic Treaty Organization. Communist insurgents were becoming active in Indochina, Malaya, the Philippines, and Greece, and a communist coup had overthrown the democratic government of Czechoslovakia. Finally, the Soviets blockaded Berlin, and China fell to the communist forces of Mao Tse-tung.

The Soviet Union exploded a nuclear device in 1949. England became a nuclear power in 1952, and France followed about a decade later.[3] Since then, those nations that do not have nuclear weapons are not precluded by money or technology from developing them. Nuclear weapons are now a bargain in the weapons arsenal. It was not until the mid-1960s that they became an imminent and direct threat to every nation by virtue of the development of intercontinental ballistic missile delivery capability.

First the Korean War and then the Suez crisis placed the world on the brink of nuclear war in the 1950s. Disagreements among the NATO allies, triggered by competition among the allies for weapons sales, by questions of sovereignty, by internal difficulties such as the Ulster rebellions in Great Britain, and by the Korean War and civil rights movements in the United States, contributed to a decline in the preparedness of NATO forces. France, under President Charles de Gaulle, became particularly sensitive to questions of national sovereignty. Simple language differences were a constant source of embarrassment and discord. In addition, the formidable power differential between the United States and its allies made it difficult to achieve harmony.[4]

Although NATO has often been subsidiary to the central

3. Ibid., p. 5.
4. Ibid., p. 21.

negotiations between the Soviet Union and the United States, NATO and its Soviet counterpart, the Warsaw Pact, are as central to the maintenance of world peace as is the nuclear balance between the superpowers. Soviet occupation of Eastern Europe at the end of World War II led to the establishment of communist governments in Soviet-occupied Poland, Romania, Hungary, Bulgaria, Yugoslavia, Albania, and East Germany.[5]

Soviet concerns over the rearmament of West Germany and its admission to NATO in 1955 precipitated the formation of the Warsaw Pact. The preamble of the Warsaw Pact agreement states that "the situation created in Europe by the ratification of the Paris agreements, which envisage the formation of a new military alignment in the shape of a 'Western European Union,' with the participation of a remilitarized Western Germany and the integration of the latter in the North-Atlantic bloc, which increases the danger of another war and constitutes a threat to the national security of peaceable states" makes the defensive alliance necessary.[6] Eight countries approved the agreement on May 14, 1955: Albania, Bulgaria, Czechoslovakia, East Germany, Hungary, Poland, Romania, and the Soviet Union.[7]

Although the language of the two alliance charters is very similar, their actual functioning differs considerably. Whereas the United States, perhaps necessarily, plays a dominant role in the NATO alliance, the organization is an autonomous body, and the United States by no means has a controlling interest or authority in its decisions. On the other hand, the Warsaw Pact alliance functions as a direct extension of the Soviet Union's foreign policy and military establishment. Canadian foreign minister Lester Pearson describes the NATO alliance as a "voluntary coalition of free countries." In contrast, he says, the Warsaw Pact was imposed on the Soviet Union's satellites without any request for popular approval or referendum. The Soviet Union can at any time impose its will on the members of the coalition, whereas the United States

5. Robert W. Clawson and Lawrence S. Kaplan, eds., *The Warsaw Pact: Political Purpose and Military Means* (Wilmington, Del.: Scholarly Resources, 1982), p. 69.
6. Ibid., p. 68.
7. Ibid.

cannot, "without great difficulty."[8] In fact, any attempt by the
United States to impose its will on the alliance might very
well lead to the dismemberment of the alliance, and thus the
United States has generally tried to maintain the profile of
an equal partner. Given the formidable resources of the NATO
member nations and the changing structures of military power,
U.S. strength is much closer to its allies now than it probably
was when NATO was founded.

Although many analysts have concluded that the Warsaw
Pact is an extension of the Soviet totalitarian military state,
its importance as a strategic military buffer zone has never
been questioned. After World War II, Soviet occupation of
Eastern Europe was designed to construct a buffer between
Europe and the Soviet Union, such that another invasion of
Soviet soil might never occur. Soviet occupation and control
of that buffer was established by the end of 1948, but the Warsaw Pact legitimized the control and provided a vehicle for
better coordination.

The Soviet Union's launch of the first man-made satellite
in October, 1957, followed by the U.S. launch of a satellite in
January, 1958, changed the priorities and concerns of the Soviet bloc and of the Western alliance. These launches increased
the danger of a direct confrontation between the two superpowers. The Soviet Union began to lower troop strength in
Europe under the assumption that conventional warfare with
land forces was becoming obsolete. Development of larger and
more powerful nuclear weapons was given top priority. New
rounds of Soviet nuclear testing and the spread of nuclear technology created new concerns about world survival. The scientific community began to warn of the dangers of fallout and
strontium 90. Even nonhostile testing of nuclear weapons
could endanger life, especially when the weapons being tested
by the Soviet Union were in the fifty to one hundred megaton
range, completely dwarfing the power of the early World War
II atomic bombs.[9]

In 1962, world tensions heightened with a direct confrontation involving the naval forces of the United States and a So-

8. Ibid., p. 67.
9. Ben Bova, *Assured Survival* (Boston: Houghton Mifflin Company, 1984),
p. 63.

viet vessel carrying an intercontinental ballistic missile to Cuba. The United States, through air surveillance, discovered the development of Soviet missile sites in Cuba, only ninety miles from the American coast. President John F. Kennedy imposed a naval blockade of Cuba to prevent the delivery of nuclear missiles to the sites. In virtually the final moments, a Soviet vessel was ordered to turn around rather than to attempt to pass through the American blockade, which would have meant military action and probably war. The Soviet Union was also forced to withdraw its missiles from Cuba. At the time, the incident was regarded as a major strategic victory for the United States and the Western alliance, but in reality it strengthened Soviet resolve to develop a superior force in intercontinental missiles and warheads.

Nevertheless, the very real peril of nuclear war and the clear dangers even of "peaceful" nuclear testing led in 1963 to the Limited Nuclear Test Ban Treaty, approved by the Soviet Union, the United States, and the United Kingdom. The treaty banned the testing of nuclear weapons in the atmosphere, the ocean, or in space. Thereafter, it was to be conducted below the surface of the earth; missile testing has presumably been with dummy warheads. A 1967 treaty prohibited the deployment of nuclear weapons in space, and in 1969 another agreement limited the number of antiballistic missiles that could be deployed by the Soviet Union and the United States. Although the three powers ceased atmospheric testing, underground tests continued and missile and warhead design quickened. By the close of the 1960s, the world still seemed poised on the brink of nuclear disaster. For these and for a variety of other reasons, by the close of the 1960s the strong movement for peace and nuclear disarmament that began early in the decade produced a Soviet-American detente and serious arms control negotiations.

The product of this detente was the Strategic Arms Limitation Talks agreement (SALT) between the United States and the Soviet Union, completed on May 26, 1972. The agreement froze the number of intercontinental ballistic missiles (ICBMs) and the number of submarine-launched ballistic missiles (SLBMs) that each side could possess at the number then in existence or under construction as of the date of the treaty. Because of SALT, the United States maintains approximately

1,954 ICBMs with nuclear warheads and 656 submarine-launched missiles. U.S. nuclear missile levels stand at the 1966 level. The Soviet Union, which added heavily to its missile capabilities after 1966, has promised to maintain its missile levels at 1,618 silo-based intercontinental missiles and 710 submarine missiles. The SALT agreements did not regulate the number of bombers capable of carrying nuclear bombs, or the number of warheads that each missile could carry.[10]

Since SALT I, controversy between the two powers has continued over inspection of missile sites and warheads. Because the treaty did not mention the number of warheads that a single missile might carry, the Soviet Union in particular and the United States to a lesser extent developed multiple, independently targeted re-entry vehicles (MIRVs). Thus with a single launcher or missile, a number of re-entry missiles carrying warheads could be directed at innumerable targets. The theoretical limitations established by SALT I all but disappeared. The nuclear arms race, pitting most prominently the two major world powers, continued unabated.

The rising costs of military hardware in the Soviet Union and in the United States, a continuing strong peace and disarmament movement within the United States and among the citizens of allied NATO powers, and the apparent voiding of the SALT I agreements contributed to new peace initiatives by the United States. President Jimmy Carter signed the SALT II agreement in June, 1979, but it was not sent to the U.S. Senate for ratification because of the Soviet invasion of Afghanistan.[11]

The SALT II agreements were to have limited the total number of launch vehicles as well as the number of warheads that each power could possess. They were widely criticized because of the alleged difficulty of proving compliance by either side. Nevertheless, until 1986 the United States chose to conform to the terms of the agreement, expecting the Soviet Union to do the same. In 1982, the latter accepted the principle of on-site inspections.[12] That, with the capability of the United

---

10. For an interesting commentary on the SALT negotiations from the Soviet point of view, read Arkady N. Shevchenko, *Breaking with Moscow* (New York: Alfred A. Knopf, 1985), esp. pp. 201–206; see also Gerard Smith, *Doubletalk: The Story of SALT* (New York: Doubleday, 1980).

11. Shevchenko, *Breaking with Moscow*, p. 299.

12. See Smith, *Doubletalk*; although much has been written on the Viet-

States and possibly of the Soviet Union to detect missile deployment and sites through "spy" satellite systems does give the SALT II agreements some degree of control and verification.

Another by-product of the Cuban missile crisis, the Nuclear Test Ban Treaty and the SALT agreements was to return Soviet attention to strengthening conventional armaments and troop strength in the Warsaw Pact zone. In addition, it devoted new energies to the expansion of its submarine and surface naval forces. Antisatellite weapons and new and more powerful and accurate warheads were introduced into the Warsaw Pact arsenal. The United States, meanwhile, was preoccupied with war in Vietnam. The Soviet Union was generally successful in upgrading and strengthening its nuclear arsenal throughout the 1970s, without real violation of the SALT I agreements.

In 1977, the Soviet Union introduced its "new generation" SS-20 missiles, a medium-range ballistic missile that seemed to give it and the Warsaw Pact nations a decided advantage over the NATO alliance. The ability of NATO to respond effectively to a first strike by Warsaw Pact missiles and armies became questionable. If there were doubts about the ability of the Western alliance to retaliate to a first strike, then the deterrent effect of Western military strength was decidedly lowered, and the possibility of war greater. One response was the development of the Pershing II cruise missiles and their eventual deployment in the mid-1980s.[13]

The deterrent or defensive capabilities of the NATO military forces compared to Warsaw Pact forces have been much debated. Comparative data on troop strength, armament, and weapons indicate a critical superiority by Warsaw Pact military forces over those of the North Atlantic Treaty Organization. Although the statistics will often vary somewhat, the data published by the Washington, D.C.-based Committee on the Present Danger in 1984 indicate the gap between NATO and Warsaw Pact forces (see table 4).

A 1984 NATO study also concludes that Warsaw Pact forces maintain a decided lead over the Western alliance. Although

---

nam War, an excellent review is Harrison E. Salisbury, *Vietnam Reconsidered: Lesson from a War* (New York: Harper and Row, 1984).

13. A popular but sound treatment of Soviet military forces and weapons is Andrew Cockburn, *The Threat: Inside the Soviet Military Machine* (New York: Vintage Books, 1983), esp. pp. 295–353.

Table 4   Comparative Military Strength, NATO and Warsaw Pact

	NATO	Warsaw Pact
Total military forces	4,500,000	6,000,000
Division equivalents	115	192
Main battle tanks	17,730	46,230
Antitank guided weapons	19,170	35,400
Artillery/mortars	14,700	38,800
Armored personnel carriers	39,580	94,800
Attack helicopters	900	1,175
Transport helicopters	6,000	1,375

Source: Committee on the Present Danger, *Can America Catch Up?* (Washington, D.C., 1984), p. 43.

NATO has retired some of its older nuclear missile weapons, the deployment of new systems has been slow, and "the Warsaw Pact shows a continuing build-up of their nuclear forces across the entire spectrum. In Europe, the Warsaw Pact has an advantage over NATO in all major categories of nuclear forces."[14] The figures in table 5 indicate the comparative nuclear strength of Warsaw Pact and NATO forces.

Secretary of Defense Caspar Weinberger says that in evaluating comparative combat potential of the opposing forces and considering troop numbers and the quality of weapons, it would appear that the Warsaw Pact forces were strengthened by 90 percent between 1965 and 1984, whereas NATO forces improved by less than 40 percent.[15] It is nonetheless unclear what the widening gap between the military capabilities of the NATO and Warsaw Pact alliances portends, or if there really is a critical weakness in the defensive capabilities of the NATO forces.

The level of NATO preparedness may not be as low as the figures suggest. Military strategists generally accept the rule of thumb that defensive forces can withstand attacks of up to three times their own strength. As a defensive force, NATO armies are statistically equal or possibly slightly superior to the forces deployed against them. Another consideration is

14. Committee on the Present Danger, *Can America Catch Up?* (Washington, D.C.: 1984), pp. 33–35.
15. Ibid., p. 55.

Table 5   Comparative Nuclear Strength, Warsaw Pact and NATO

| | | WARSAW PACT | | | |
Missile	Warheads	Range (km)	Mode	Total	When Operational
SS-4	1	2,000	Fixed	224	late 1950s
SS-5	1	4,100	Fixed	13	early 1960s
SS-20	3 MIRV	c.5,000	Mobile	378	1977

| | | NATO | | | |
Missile	Warheads	Range (km)	Mode	Total	When Operational
Pershing II	1	1,800	Mobile	9	1983
GLCM	1	2,500	Mobile	32	1983

Source: Committee on the Present Danger, *Can America Catch Up?* p. 35.
Note: The statistics represent the number of missiles on launchers and are the longer-range missile systems deployed at the end of 1983.

the likelihood that an attack by Warsaw Pact forces against NATO would immediately precipitate nuclear war before such an attack could be fully mobilized. Thus, the NATO ground forces are considered in this context as a hostage to prevent or discourage offensive acts by the Warsaw Pact nations.

Neither can the military balance of power be determined by a simple comparison of the relative strengths and weaknesses of the NATO and Warsaw Pact forces. The outbreak of war in Europe must inevitably involve military responses and repercussions throughout the world. What China, Japan, and Southeast Asia might do is uncertain. Whatever action they might take would have a great bearing on the result of any war between the Eastern and Western alliances, between the United States and the Soviet Union. Israel and the Mid-East could also directly influence the outcome of war in Europe. The hazards and uncertainties of any future war themselves deter the outbreak of war in Europe and elsewhere.

Nuclear weapons, which could include the catastrophic neutron bombs, and conventional military forces would not likely be the only factors at issue in future warfare. Future weapons may well exceed the capabilities and sophistication of those now known. Nothing has changed so rapidly in the age of high tech than the weapons or potential weapons of war.

Advanced Weapons Systems

Naval Weapons

The United States and the Soviet Union, as well as France and England, have developed modern navies that include nuclear submarines and surface ships and nuclear-powered aircraft carriers. In addition to these basic structural developments, weapons systems have been refined and improved through the application of electronic and computer technology.

The United States naval weapons systems, for example, now include the AEGIS system, which provides guidance and control for surface-to-air missiles launched from destroyers and cruisers. These guided missiles, using conventional warheads, have a high performance capability against aircraft and surface- or subsurface-launched antiship missiles. The Naval Tactical Data System (NTDS) is a combination of digital computers, displays, and transmission links that increases an individual ship commander's capability to assess tactical data and take action. It integrates information from various sensors (radar, sonar, and so on) and provides displays of tactical situations and the defense or offense options available. PHALANX is a rapid-fire, short-range gun system being developed to provide defense against antiship missiles. PHALANX can theoretically deliver up to three thousand rounds of 20mm ammunition per minute from a six-barrel "gatling gun" arrangement aimed and fired by five electronic fire-control systems.[16] What one hears of most often, however, are the supercarriers and nuclear submarine forces.

American supercarriers are nuclear powered and are the largest ships afloat today. Indeed, they are so large that many authorities consider them highly vulnerable. Others suggest that they are far less vulnerable than land-based aircraft facilities located in any part of the world, including the United States. The floating airfields can service about ninety military aircraft and represent the United States' primary attack capability, short of intercontinental nuclear missiles. These

---

16. Capt. John R. W. Moore, ed., *Jane's Fighting Ships, 1984–1985* (New York: Jane's Publishing, 1984), pp. 155, 636.

ships, with the Trident missiles and the new Ohio-class submarine, give the United States a clear superiority over Soviet naval strength. The Soviet Union, however, has made tremendous strides in developing a formidable, modern navy, including nuclear surface and submarine vessels.

The Soviet submarine force carrying long-range ballistic missiles has probably exceeded the level of American submarine forces. The Soviet Union has for approximately a decade launched six or seven nuclear-powered submarines each year. The newest, the Typhoon class, is the largest submarine ever launched, almost double the displacement of its rivals. It is capable of operating anywhere in the world and has access to any target in the world from wherever it is located.[17]

The Soviet navy has emphasized the construction of mid-sized surface ships, rather than the super-class ship. Most of its modern ships are cruisers, destroyers, and frigates. The Soviet Union currently operates four conventionally powered aircraft carriers of the Kiev class and has a nuclear-powered carrier scheduled for launch early in the next decade. The electronic and computer control systems for naval weapons are not believed to have reached the sophisticated levels of those developed by the United States, but there is constant improvement and upgrading.

The United Kingdom and France have independent naval forces with nuclear power and nuclear weapons capabilities. Despite the impressive naval developments of the Soviet Union over the past few decades, the Western alliance retains, at least collectively, naval superiority.

Airpower

Whereas capital ships, that is, ships of the tonnage of heavy cruisers, battleships, and aircraft carriers, were the primary index of military power in the period leading up to World War I and, for most military strategists, the major power index through World War II, airpower has tended to displace seapower since World War II. Although it is conceded that air forces, using nonnuclear weapons, may not win a war, it is generally believed that an air force can neutralize a superior ground force.

---

17. Ibid., p. 497; and see Ronald T. Pretty, ed., *Jane's Weapon Systems, 1982–1983* (New York: Jane's Publishing, 1982) pp. 2–20.

Since the 1950s, improvements in military aircraft have largely been in design and in the electronics surveillance and weapons control systems. The United States has constantly improved the versatility of its AWACS (Airborne Warning and Control Systems). The system is essentially a mobile, high-capacity radar station and a command, control, and communications station. A number of them remain aloft constantly in Boeing 707 aircraft frames. AWACS provide surveillance of all air vehicles, "manned or unmanned, and [provide] detection, tracking and identification capability during all weather and above all kinds of terrain."[18] The AWACS Sentry crew of seventeen can provide safe communications battle links to as many as ninety-eight thousand different NATO units.[19]

Development is continuing on the B1-B bomber, which is designed to supersede the aging B-52 aircraft. The B-1B is designed to enhance the airborne leg of the U.S. nuclear triad. The aircraft is designed with increased hardness against nuclear blast effects and has a smaller radar cross-section to increase its survivability in case of a Soviet first strike. It will be equipped with the new generation of air-launched cruise missiles to increase its strategic effectiveness. Given the reluctance of Congress to fully fund the construction of these ninety-million-dollar aircraft, it is very possible that the B1-B bomber will become history before it ever becomes operational. The United States is also currently at work on a "high technology" bomber called the Stealth, which incorporates electronic jamming devices, radar-absorbent materials, and exotic configurations to produce electronic "invisibility."

Despite the tragic loss of the *Challenger* in January, 1986, earlier successes with space shuttle operations suggest that aircraft and spacecraft design may become more similar. Although conventional aircraft are unlikely to become obsolete, for certain military purposes the high-altitude bomber may well be superseded by craft that could operate within or outside the earth's atmosphere.

In the past decade the Soviet Union has outpaced the United States in the number of new military aircraft designs deployed

18. John W. R. Taylor, ed., *All the World's Aircraft: Jane's 82–83* (New York: Jane's Publishing, 1984), p. 155.
19. Ibid.

each year. Between 1973 and 1982, it built six thousand tactical aircraft, compared to three thousand built by the United States. Soviet fighter/attack aircraft development has been equally impressive. The MiG-29, Su-27, and the latest MiG-31 are each faster than their American-made counterparts and now include sophisticated look-down, shoot-down radar tracking systems.

The new Tupolev-class bomber, known as the Blackjack, is designed to counter the American B1-B. It will have air-launched cruise missiles that can be launched at targets from within Soviet airspace.[20] The Soviet Union also unveiled a very impressive super transport aircraft, the An-124, in Paris in 1985. Aircraft design and capability are changing rapidly. It is unlikely that any of the aircraft currently deployed will be militarily effective in a decade or two.

Ground Forces

The Soviet Union has generally pursued a somewhat different course in modernizing and upgrading conventional ground weapons systems. Whereas the United States spends a longer period refining a new weapon before deploying it, the Soviet Union will ordinarily develop a weapon and rapidly deploy it, making refinements later as they become warranted. The costs of American field weapons will, as a result, often be substantially greater than those used by Soviet forces, but in theory the quality of American weapons is superior. There is, however, no question but that the Soviet Union maintains troop and armament superiority over the United States and its allies.

Because of the Soviet commitment to a highly mobile but heavily armed attack force, the country has concentrated on the development of tanks, helicopters, assault vehicles, and mobile artillery launchers. Western military strategy is in part guided by an elaborate "Air Land Battle 2000" concept, developed by the U.S. Army Training and Development Command (TRADOC) which assumes the invasion of the West by Warsaw Pact forces. The attack strategy presumably incorporates elements of the World War II German blitzkrieg tactics with a broader concept of correlating air and land forces of varying types to accomplish specific battle objectives. In this theory,

20. Ibid., p. 228.

the important first battle would determine the subsequent battle plans and probably the outcome of the war.

Whereas the Soviet Union concentrates on the development of attack capabilities and equipment, the United States and NATO give major attention to the development of effective armor-defense weapons. Development, for example, continues on a laser-guided antitank missile that can be fired from a new large class of Apache helicopter, or from the new Bradley personnel carrier. A new generation of artillery shells incorporates laser tracking to direct the shell to its target. The advanced M-1 tank includes the latest in electronic targeting. Smart bombs and night vision are part of the paraphernalia of modern land warfare, as are small personal rocket-launching devices and guided bazooka shells. It is anticipated that in the foreseeable future Soviet forces will maintain superiority in troops deployed and in conventional weapons, but that the United States will concentrate on the development of new high-tech weapons.[21]

Future Weapons

Some of the weapons of the future are already here, although they likely will be refined in a variety of ways. The technology of missiles and nuclear warheads is unlikely to change much over the next three or more decades. What is not here yet, but probably will be in the not too distant future, is "smart" weapons, programmed to complete a certain task or destroy a given target, as well as armed satellites, laser weapons, particle beams, rail guns, and "Buck Rogers" devices. The Strategic Defense Initiative envisioned by the Reagan administration is, perhaps, a harbinger of things to come.

Admittedly, even if most people knew what these future weapons were to be, few would be able to comprehend them, although the objectives and intended results would likely be quite clear. Most military research on nuclear weapons has been conducted in government laboratories such as those at Los Alamos and Sandia, New Mexico. Aerospace research and development has generally been carried out by private firms such as Grumman, McDonnell-Douglas, Boeing, Pratt and

21. Committee on the Present Danger, *Can America Catch Up?* p. 44.

Whitney, Bell Laboratories, and General Dynamics. Some research and development is also conducted in public and private universities. It is estimated that in 1984 aerospace research and development costs were $17.9 billion.[22]

Jane's Aerospace Dictionary offers the general reader the most accurate description and classification of existing ballistic missiles. The following terms offer some insight into the world of nuclear war potential:

Abbreviation	Description
ABM	Antiballistic missile, capable of intercepting re-entry vehicles (ICBMs)
A/S	Air/surface classification
ASM	Air-to-surface missile, guided with propulsion, launched from air against land or sea targets
ICBM	Intercontinental ballistic missile
IRBM	Intermediate-range ballistic missile
MIRV	Multiple, independently targeted re-entry vehicle
MRBM	Medium-range, or mid-range ballistic missile
RV	Re-entry vehicle
SAM	Surface-to-air missile
SLBM	Submarine-launched ballistic missile

A thermonuclear weapon is defined as a device for which fission provides high temperature for the fusion of nuclei of hydrogen isotopes. Throw weight is the total mass of a payload carried by a ballistic missile, which in the case of an ICBM would include "warheads, RV's, decoys and other penaids, and post boost propulsion and terminal guidance systems."[23] The language of modern warfare is high-tech language.

It may be useful to examine some of the known quantities of nuclear-ballistic warfare. It may also be useful to remember that the nuclear age is now only fifty years old. The largest known nuclear arsenals are those of the United States, France,

22. Aerospace Industries Association of America, *Aerospace Facts and Figures, 1984–1985* (New York: Aviation Week and Space Technology Publishers, 1984), p. 110.
23. *Jane's Aerospace Dictionary* (New York: Jane's Publishing, 1984).

England, and the Soviet Union. The United States, so far as is known, leads the NATO alliance in research, development, and deployment of nuclear weapons systems.

Expectations are that the United States will continue to emphasize the development of smaller, more mobile missiles with increasingly accurate guidance systems. These will include missile-defense penetration aids, that is, electronic devices intended to confuse or divert intercept missiles, and computer-assisted delivery systems to enhance accuracy and the probability of reaching the target.[24] As existing nuclear weapons systems become obsolete, the United States will be forced to choose between modifying those systems or developing new ones. Recent trends in defense procurement indicate that the latter might be more likely to occur. Budgetary constraints and changes in national leadership could affect defense decisions.[25]

The United States has a large number of nuclear weapons systems scheduled for development and deployment in the near future. The Minuteman III is a MIRV that delivers three thermonuclear warheads with a force of 330 kilotons each. It features a four-stage ICBM, multiple warheads, decoys, and advanced guidance and propulsion systems. The proposed MX missile would be a four-stage ICBM with a range of fourteen thousand kilometers, delivering ten thermonuclear bombs of 450 kilotons each. A low-level GLCM (guided low-altitude continental or short-range missile) is a short-range missile with a very sophisticated guidance system that delivers a single thermonuclear warhead approximately twelve hundred miles. The Trident II missiles would replace the Trident I and contain a larger payload of approximately 100 kilotons, have a range of four thousand, six hundred miles, and be capable of evasive maneuvers.[26]

The development of strategic nuclear weapons in the Soviet Union has followed a somewhat different pattern from that of the United States, France, and Britain. As in the case of conventional weapons, the Soviet Union does not devote

24. "U.S. Army Plan: Keep Talking, Keep Building," *U.S. News and World Report* (February 18, 1985): 23.
25. Ibid.
26. Ibid.; see also *Jane's Weapon Systems, 1982–1983*, pp. 11–20; and Cockburn, *Soviet Threat*, p. 9.

unusual effort and expense to prototype development and testing. Production of the missile begins while testing continues. This modification process allows the Soviets to continue production while adjusting the missile's characteristics to meet new strategic requirements.

The Soviet SS-18 intercontinental-range ballistic missile offers a good example of production and deployment practices. Originally deployed in 1974 to replace the SS-9 missile, there have been four models developed since then, the latest of which was deployed in 1982. Improvements in the original occurred as follows:[27]

Missile	Warheads	Yield	Range (miles)	Year Deployed
SS-18, Mod 2	8	900 KT	6,800	1977
SS-18, Mod 3	1	20 MT	6,500	1979
SS-18, Mod 4	10	50 KT	6,800	1982

The latest development has been the rapid deployment of the SS-20 missile. It was designed to take the place of aging SS-4 and SS-5 ICBMs. This new-generation missile incorporates state-of-the-art guidance systems and is more mobile. Greater mobility enhances the chance of the missile's surviving an attack.

Given the very real likelihood of another war's involving attacks from re-entry vehicles, or even from stationary space platforms, there have been some calls for treaties that would ban the militarization of space. Since the introduction of Nazi Germany's V-2 rocket, the military use of space has grown considerably to include communication and reconnaissance satellites and the testing of large ballistic missile systems that pierce the atmosphere to deliver their warheads. Space laboratories have been in orbit for weeks or months conducting various scientific and possibly military-related tests for Soviet and American authorities.

The use of reconnaissance satellites has become an integral part of military intelligence for both superpowers, particularly for the United States. Troop movements, weapons development, and nuclear missile verification are only part of the information gathered through such reconnaissance.

27. *Jane's Weapon Systems,* pp. 4–9.

Satellites can provide strategic information on weather conditions, crops, and mining operations. The KH-11 is reputed to be one of the most advanced American reconnaissance satellites. It was launched on December 19, 1976, after more than five years of development. It is six stories tall, weighs fifteen tons, and is alleged to be the state-of-the-art espionage satellite. The KH-11 uses television lenses and transmission, which sometimes produces images with less clarity and resolution than older, film-using models, such as the KH-9 (or Big Bird) and the KH-8. The film models continue in service but require servicing at nine- and 4-month intervals, respectively.[28] One might also presume that the more that is publicly known about a particular reconnaissance satellite's performance, the less likely it is in fact to be a state-of-the-art piece of equipment.

As far as can be determined, Soviet technological advances in reconnaissance satellite production lag significantly behind U.S. development. Space technology is one of the few areas in which the Soviet Union continues to trail the United States. Defense specialist James Bamford says that the Soviets are still relying on satellites that return the film in capsules rather than on instant-time video monitors. They were forced to launch twenty-seven photo satellites in 1983, compared with the two launched by the United States.[29] There are recent indications that the Soviets are now employing new video transmitters in their satellites, since the latest one launched has been in operation for an extended period.

Very likely some of the recent advances in Soviet reconnaissance resulted from theft of American technology. William Kampiles, a former CIA employee, is known to have sold Soviet agents the KH-11 technical manual. Another spy, Christopher Boyce, a former TRW employee (whose company helped develop the KH-11, sold information on U.S. satellite development to Soviet agents. (That espionage saga is the subject of a book and a movie, *The Falcon and the Snowman*.)

The next generation of reconnaissance satellites is expected to include radar-image capabilities that allow the "eye" to see

28. James Bamford, "America's Supersecret Eyes in Space," *New York Times Magazine* (January 13, 1985), p. 51.
29. Ibid.

through cloud cover. Supersensitive eavesdropping satellites are also being developed and are designed to track and gather communications data. According to Bamford, the radar satellite would orbit at an altitude of 22,300 miles and remain "parked" in a single spot over the earth. It could see through cloud cover and other weather conditions and transmit what it sees instantly. The communications satellites or "ferrets," he says, could hear everything from radar to long-distance telephone calls to the high-pitched whistle of telemetry from a missile test.[30]

One of the most remarkable proposals, and one that has very serious potential, in part because it has the strong support of the president of the United States, is the Strategic Defense Initiative (SDI) system. This system envisions a space-based defense against nuclear missile attack. In an address on March 23, 1983, President Reagan outlined the SDI, popularly called the "star wars" defense initiative, as a proposed research project. Preliminary investigation has since begun. The concept itself is important, even before the development of any models or hardware. SDI marks a departure from the doctrine of mutually assured destruction (MAD) to a real defensive posture. The concept also brings into question possible testing in violation of SALT I and II and the Nuclear Test Ban Treaty. Even admitting the "right" to develop such defensive capabilities, SDI could destabilize current military balances and understandings.

Those who support SDI argue that at present it is only a research initiative and involves a feasibility study of a space-based defense against nuclear weapons. No real conclusions can be drawn until data are gathered and new information tested. It is also argued that SDI offers the opportunity for significant research in laser development, particle-beam systems, fourth-generation computer operations, and advanced tracking and monitoring systems. Scientists suggest, too, that the development of such a system supports and complements the space shuttle program. Some analysts also justify American development on the grounds that the Soviets have already violated current arms treaties and are working on a space-based defense of their own. Most important, SDI envisions

30. Ibid., p. 52.

a nonaggressive defense weapon. As science fiction writer Ben Bova describes it, "By using the new techniques of warfare suppression the world can move from the era of MADness into an era of Mutual Assured Survival."[31]

Arguments against the development of SDI are that it could destabilize world power structures and prompt the Soviets into a preemptive strike. We have avoided nuclear catastrophe and military hostilities between the major powers for the past fifty years. In addition, SDI would likely initiate a new and terribly expensive weapons race. The system, some believe, is simply not feasible and, even if put in place, would soon become obsolete. Finally, any developments along the lines of space-based defense mechanisms will be challenged as a violation of treaty commitments.[32]

Initial thought about a space-based defense system concludes that it would involve three layers of weapons. The first would be a wave of orbiting satellites that would destroy nuclear missiles in their boost phase. The satellites would locate the attacking missiles immediately after launch, when the heat from their rockets makes them easy to spot. Calculations of trajectory and speed of the attacking missiles would take only nanoseconds (a billionth of a second) as the fourth-generation on-board computers of the satellites tracked and destroyed the majority of the launched missiles.

The second layer of defense would be another wave of defense satellites that would track and destroy most of the remaining missiles in much the same fashion as did the first. Tracking would be more difficult, however, because the boost phase would have been completed and the missile would presumably contain "decoys" to confuse the defense system. However, because most of the launched missiles would already have been destroyed, the second-tier defense mechanisms would be able to destroy most of the remaining attack missiles.

The final defense would be a layer of ground-based anti-ballistic missiles. These ABM systems would be strategically located and would track and destroy incoming missiles as they reached the upper atmosphere. It is hoped that by destroying

31. Bova, *Assured Survival*, inside cover.
32. Lt. Gen. Daniel O. Graham, USA (Ret.), Project Director, *High Frontier Study: A Summary* (Washington, D.C.: High Frontier, 1982), p. 8.

most of the missiles in the original launch phase, the second and third layers of defense satellites would have the time to track and destroy most of those that remained. Unfortunately, no system is foolproof. SDI, some believe, would strengthen the deterrent factors for nuclear war, because the probable failure of a nuclear attack would mean massive retaliation. If such failure is viewed as a real threat, however, the great danger of SDI is that it could precipitate a preemptive strike before the system could become operational.

There has also been speculation that some of the defensive missiles might be better armed by laser devices or particle beams. They would be guided by very advanced heat-seeking guidance systems. One group has proposed a "High Frontier" concept, which would utilize existing ABM designs but would deploy them on fixed satellites. The satellites would carry multiple missiles (as many as forty-five) and on-board computers to monitor, calculate, and project the trajectory of the targets and the antimissiles. The satellites would also begin to serve as a command, control, and communications (C^3) system. Supporters believe such a system could be fully deployed in as little as five years at a cost of some ten to fifteen billion dollars.[33]

One of the more advanced technologies being studied for possible use as a weapon on space-based defense satellites is the laser. Laser is an acronym for light amplification by stimulated emission of radiation. "Light" refers not only to visible light, but also to the whole spectrum of electromagnetic energy. This includes radio waves, infrared, visible, ultraviolet, x-rays, and gamma rays, with radio waves being the least powerful and gamma rays possessing the greatest intensity.

A laser beam is a concentrated and intense point of energy. For example, the sun emits seven kilowatts of energy per square centimeter. Laser beams have been developed to focus more than ten billion watts of energy on a square centimeter. Lasers can also maintain their focus or direction over great distances. Very low power laser beams have been bounced off the moon and have dispersed to only a mile in diameter after a trip of a quarter of a million miles.[34]

33. Ibid.
34. Bova, *Assured Survival*, p. 331.

Recent research in laser technology has been intense and productive. Dr. Edward Teller, the father of the atomic bomb, is examining x-ray lasers in the Livermore National Laboratory in California. The x-ray laser is the most lethal under development. Gamma ray lasers have not yet been created. The x-ray laser can focus sufficient energy to destroy an ICBM. According to Dr. Teller, such a laser can be created by the power of a relatively small nuclear explosion, about one-twentieth the size of the Hiroshima bomb, with the energy focused through a working medium of gas, which will emit the x-ray beam. It is anticipated that a single satellite armed with the x-ray laser and an advanced tracking system could track and destroy a large number of attacking missiles. Countermeasures, however, might be relatively simple and cheap devices such as reflector surfaces, aerosol gases, dust particles, mechanical rotation, or electronic shielding.

In part because of the suspected fallibility of laser guns, there is considerable interest in the development of particle beams, which would be less easily diverted or destroyed. Particle beams are formed by accelerating subatomic particles such as electrons and protons at speeds approaching 186,000 miles per second, the speed of light. The particles are placed in an electromagnetic field accelerator, which is formed by using extremely powerful electromagnets and high-voltage generators. The subatomic particles are pushed or pulled, depending on their charge, and accelerate to their maximum speeds before leaving the accelerator. The beam is then directed at the target, where it smashes into the surface and releases an enormous destructive force.

The development of particle-beam weapons in space-based missile defense is inhibited in that the particles must be neutralized before the beam can be directed. Researchers believe that this can be done by accelerating positively charged protons through a field of negatively charged electrons. The protons, weighing 1,837 times more than electrons, would be able to maintain velocity while being neutralized. The energy requirements for the generators used to accelerate the particles are enormous and would presumably require atomic explosions similar to those envisioned for x-ray lasers.[35] Once gen-

35. Ibid., pp. 334–36.

erated, the particle beam would be far less susceptible to diversion or dissolution than would the laser beam.

An interesting derivative of the particle-beam concept is the "rail gun," which would accelerate heavier projectiles, or "flechettes," along an electromagnetic rail and literally hurl the projectile at a target at speeds up to fifty thousand miles per hour. Test models of rail guns have been built that can hurl plastic cubes along copper rails at velocities approaching three miles per second. The rails are powered by short bursts of twenty-five hundred megawatts of electricity. Even a plastic cube hurled at a velocity of five miles per second could penetrate the quarter-inch steel plates commonly used to shield components of intercontinental ballistic missiles.[36] Although an adaptation of a rail gun might conceivably be mounted on a defensive satellite, one might also be used to hurl bulk cargoes into space at an extremely low cost as compared to space shuttle launches.

One of the great attractions of military research on space weapons and defense is that such research will also yield rewards for the scientific and civilian sectors. Just as atomic energy began as a war effort and became a technology for the generation of consumer power, so it is hoped, the high-technology of future wars that we hope will never be will generate greater world security and improved human welfare.

Conclusions

The decision to develop and use weapons is not primarily a military decision; it is largely a political and social decision that must be tempered by religious values and educated guesses and that will be determined in part by economic realities. That is to say, the world of the future is an interdependent and interrelated world in terms of its physical geography and its people, but also in terms of the cultural milieu in which people live. That culture is a combination of a people's political beliefs and structures, its social values and organization, its educational and informational development, its economy, its religious and philosophical systems, and its physical or military power. One aspect of culture cannot really be isolated

36. Ibid., pp. 340–41; *Houston Chronicle* (November 11, 1985), pp. 1–6.

from the other. Thus, what happens in the future will be the product of all of the factors that we have examined, the military future no less so than any other.

The conferences between President Ronald Reagan and Soviet leader Mikhail S. Gorbachev in Geneva in November, 1985, are still having an effect on arms control, space defense, scientific research, national economies in both East and West, and world security. Heraclitus seems to have been correct in observing that "nothing endures but change." In no era of human history has there been as much change as in the recent past, nor as much as is likely in the postindustrial era of the next half century. Perhaps what has changed most of all is, in fact, our attitude toward change, toward technology, and toward the future. In that lies our greatest hope.

Index

Africa, 18–19, 121, 142–43
Afro-Americans, 60
aging, 54–59
agriculture, 31, 99. *See also* food;
    famine
Aid to Families with Dependent
    Children, 133
airpower, 163–65. *See also* missiles
Alfonsín, Raúl, 136
*American Education: A National
    Failure,* 118
American Lutheran Church, 71
Americans for Democratic Action,
    129
America Revisited, 46
Aokie, Hiroaki, 63
Argentina, 10, 31, 135
Asia, 19, 60, 139
Asian-Americans, 63–66
Asians, 60–66
Assembly of God, 71
atomic energy, 22

baby boomers, 125, 130
Bamford, James, 170
banking, 6, 9, 10
Baran, Joshua, 90
Barnard, Henry, 98–99
Barret, William, 43
Beyond Liberal and Conservative, 129

Birch, David, 24
birth control, 82
birth rate, 105
black families, 62–63
Black Family Summit, 50
blacks, 36, 49, 60–66; education of,
    61–62; as mayors, 61–62; in
    South Africa, 137–38; in state
    legislatures, 62
Bloesch, Donald G., 77
Bourgeois-Pichat, Jean, 55
Bova, Ben, 172
Boyce, Christopher, 170
Brazil, 10, 31, 136–37
Briggs, Kenneth A., 76–77
Brownfeld, Allan C., 95
Brun, Rev. Carol Joyce, 83
Buchwald, Rabbi Ephraim, 84
Buddhism, 77
Bureau of the Census. *See* U.S.
    Census Bureau. *See also* cen-
    sus; demography; population

Caddell, Patrick, 134–35
California, 37, 43, 63, 65, 114, 174;
    politics in, 128–29; University
    of, 55, 73, 88, 113
Canada, 128
Caribbean: industrial activity in,
    30

Carlsson, Roine, 142
Carter, Jimmy, 12, 125, 132, 158
Castro, Fidel, 64, 146
Catholicism. *See* Roman Catholicism
census, 42, 49, 60. *See also* demography; population
Center for Religious Development, 77
Central America, 30, 135
Cetron, Marvin, 23–25
Challenger, 164
Cherlin, Andrew, 53
Chesterton, G. K., 95
Chicago, 49, 64; University of, 74, 84
child abuse, 41
Children of God, 88
China, 30, 128, 144–46
Chinese, 63
Christian Computer Users Association, 81
Christian Scientists, 89
Church of Jesus Christ of Latter-Day Saints. *See* Mormonism
Church of Scientology, 88–89
Clark, Kenneth, 50
cocaine, 38–39
Colombia, 136
Conway, Flo, 89
Copperman, Paul, 108
Council on Environmental Quality, 12
Covenant House, 44
crime, 36–46; and television, 41
Crimmins, Eileen, 55
Cuba, 62, 64–65, 146–47, 157–59
Cubans, 64–65
Culp, Jerome, 61
cults, 67, 86–91
Cunningham, Lawrence S., 73
Cuomo, Mario, 132

Danish Social Workers Union, 141
Dark Ghetto, 50
Death of the Past, 45
deforestation, 15
de Gaulle, Charles, 154
Democracy in America, 69

demography, 15–19, 37–66. *See also* population
Deng Xiaoping, 145–46
detente, 157
Disciples of Christ, 71
Divine Light Movement, 88
divorce, 41, 50–55
Dominican Republic, 135
Doomsday Book: 10,000 Years of Economic Crisis, 33
drugs. *See* narcotics
drunk driving, 37
Durkheim, Emile, 49

East Asia, 24, 30
Eastern Europe, 146. *See also* Warsaw Pact
Eccles, Sir John, 78
ecology, 19
economic growth, 30–34
Ecuador, 136
education, 97–120; continuing, 115–17; home, 112–13; private, 110–12
Einstein, Albert, 79, 153
Eklund, Coy G., 57
Elementary and Secondary Education Act, 109, 118
employment, 25–26
energy, 8–9, 21–22. *See also* petroleum, atomic energy; fusion
entrepreneurship, 32, 62, 65
Episcopal church, 71
Episcopalians, 70
Equitable Life Assurance Company, 57
Erlich, Paul, 18
European Common Market, 31
Evans, M. Stanton, 127

Fair Deal, 128
family, 35, 46–54; and education, 108–15
famine, 17, 19, 147
Federal Bureau of Investigation (FBI), 36
Federal Reserve Board, 6
Feingold, S. Norman, 27
fertility, 47–54

Fichter, Joseph, 69
Filipinos, 63
flextime, 28
Florida, 65
food, 17–19, 31
Forecasting International, 23
France, 23; Communist party in, 139–40; NATO and, 154–62; religion in, 68; Socialist party in, 128, 139
freedom, 135–36
Freedom Association, 141
Freedom House, 135
Free to Choose, 144
Friedman, David, 141
Friedman, Milton, 141, 144
Friedman, Rose, 144
fundamentalists, 71
Furstenberg, Frank F., Jr., 53
fusion, 22

Gallup, George, 68, 72, 110, 127, 130
Genesis Spiritual Life Center, 78
Germany, 23, 28, 128. *See also* North Atlantic Treaty Organization; Warsaw Pact; Nazis
Gingrich, Newt, 134
Gissurarson, Hannes, 141
Global 2000 Report to the President, 3, 13–15, 20–22
The Good Years: Your Life in the Twenty-first Century, 58
Gorbachev, Mikhail S., 150
Gottschalk, Rabbi Alfred, 83
Graduate Theological Union, 91
Gramm, Phil, 124
Great Awakening, 67
Great Britain, 23, 128, 140, 146; and NATO, 152–62
Great Depression, 4, 6, 47
Great Society, 128
Gross Domestic Product (GDP), 4–5, 7, 11–12, 24
Gross National Product (GNP), 9, 11, 30, 105, 125
ground forces, 165–66
Groves, Gen. Leslie, 153
Growing without Schooling, 112

Haitians, 65
Hare Krishna, 67, 88–89
Harlem, 49
Hart, Gary, 130, 134
Hart, Peter D., 134
Harvard University, 46, 63; Center for Population Studies, 84; Divinity School, 77
Hayek, Friedrich A., 142
Hebrew Theological College, 81
Hebrew Union College, 83
Henry, Carl F. H., 74
heroin, 38–39
Higher Education Act, 118
Hinduism, 77
Hiroshima, 150, 153, 174
Hispanics, 36, 60–66
The History of the Idea of Progress, 45
Hitler, Adolf, 65, 85
Hodheim, Rabbi Samuel, 85
Holt, John, 112
Hong Kong, 144, 146
Hoover Institution, 105, 128
Hsu, Ming, 63
Human Development and Growth Associates, 58
Hungary, 146

Iacocca, Lee, 132
Iceland, 141
illegitimate children, 133–34
immigrants, 60–66
immigration, 37, 103–104
Indians, 63
industrial cycle, 4–5
Industrial Revolution, 27
inflation, 5, 11
information revolution, 23
Institute of Advanced Christian Studies, 74
Institute of Behavioral Science, 39
intermarriage, 85
International Monetary Fund, 8, 11
Iowa Test of Basic Skills, 105

Jane's Aerospace Dictionary, 167
Japan, 68, 106, 128
Japanese, 63

Jefferson, Thomas, 99
Jehovah's Witnesses, 71, 89
Jessor, Richard, 39
Johns Hopkins University, 53
Joint Center for Urban Studies, 46
Judaism, 81, 84–86

Kahn, Herman, 13, 33
Kampiles, William, 170
Kelley, Dean, 71
Kemp, Jack, 134
Kennedy, John F., 157
Kissinger, Henry, 153
Korea, 30, 62
Koreans, 63
Korean War, 154

lasers, 173–74
Latin America, 19, 121; democracy in, 135–36
Limited Nuclear Test Ban Treaty, 157
Linder, Staffan Burenstam, 142
Lindsey, Robert, 64
Lipman, Aaron, 57
The Literary Hoax, 108
Little Havana, 64
Little India, 62
Livermore National Laboratory, 174
longevity. See aging
Losing Ground, 133
Lovelace, Richard, 70
Lusardo, T. J., 63
Luther, Martin, 73

McGovern, George, 133
Maeroff, Gene I., 73
Malthus, Thomas, 16
Manhattan Institute for Policy Research, 133
Manhattan Project, 153
Mann, Edward, 90
Mann, Horace, 98–99
manufacturing, 4
Mao Tse-tung, 128, 154
Marchais, George, 139
Mariam, Mengistu Haile, 147

Mariel boat people, 65
marijuana, 38–39
marriage, 41–42; and religion, 85–86
Marshall Plan, 5
Medicaid, 133
Medicare, 55
Megatrends, 23, 93
Menninger, Karl, 43
Methodists, 70. See also United Methodist church
Mexico, 10, 68
Mexico City, 15, 29
Michigan, 132
minerals, 20
minorities, 37, 60–66
missiles, 156–75
Mitterrand, François, 139, 148
Mondale, Walter, 123, 125, 130, 132, 134
money supply, 6
Moon, Rev. Sun Myung, 88
Moral Majority, 70
Mormonism, 71, 89
Morrill Land Grant College Act, 99
multinational corporations, 31
Murray, Charles, 133–34

Nagasaki, 150, 153
Naisbitt, John, 23, 93
narcotics, 38–39
National Association of Educational Progress, 101
National Commission on Excellence in Higher Education, 119
National Endowment for the Arts, 118
National Institute of Mental Health, 40
National Urban League, 50
naval weapons, 162–63
Nazis, 153, 169
New Deal, 121, 128
New York City, 36, 42–43, 64, 79, 84, 132
Nisbet, Robert, 45
Nkrumah, Kwame, 143
Nokia, Oy, 142
nonfuel minerals, 20

North Atlantic Treaty Organization (NATO), 151–61; compared to Warsaw Pact, 160–61
Nouwen, Rev. Henri, 78
nuclear power, 22
nuclear war, 150
nuclear weapons, 153–57

oil. See petroleum
oil embargo, 10
Oppenheimer, J. Robert, 153
Organization of Petroleum Exporting Countries (OPEC), 5, 21
Organization for Economic Cooperation and Development (OECD), 8

Paraguay, 135
particle beams, 174–75
Pearson, Lester, 155
Peele, Gillian, 93
Perlman, Mark, 15–16
Perot, H. Ross, 107–108
Peru, 136
petroleum, 5, 7–8, 10, 21
Phelps, John, 33
Pifer, Alan, 57–58
Pines, Burton Yale, 70
Planck, Max, 79
Plumb, J. H., 45
Policy Center on Aging, 55
politics, 121–50; international, 135–48
Pope Paul VI, 82
Popper, Sir Karl, 79
population, 15–19, 21, 46–54
Population Reference Bureau, 56
pornography, 39–41
postindustrial era, 3, 7, 22–34
prayer. See religion
Presbyterians, 70
Princeton University: Institute for Advanced Study, 153
Protestants, 69–78

Radical Departures: Desperate Detours to Growing Up, 86
rail guns, 175
Rajneesh, Bagwan Shree, 67, 90–91

reading, 100–14
Reagan, Ronald, 44, 95, 122–23, 133–34, 149–50, 176
religion, 67–96; and education, 72–74; Gallup Polls on, 68–69, 72; and membership, 71; and politics, 93–96; and science, 78–81
The Resourceful Earth, 3, 13–14, 16, 20–22
retirement, 58–59
Revel, Jean-François, 149
Rickover, Hyman G., 118
Ritter, Father Bruce, 44
Robinson, Daniel, 79
Roman Catholicism, 69, 71, 82–85, 93
Roosevelt, Franklin, 132, 153

safety, 36–38
satellite, 156. See also missiles
Schluter, Paul, 140
Scholastic Aptitude Test (SAT), 101, 119
The Second Genesis: The Coming Control of Life, 59
Seventh-Day Adventists, 71
sexual abuse, 42. See also child abuse
sexual revolution, 53–54
Simon, Julian, 13, 104–105
socialism, 148
Social Security, 123
society, 37, 60–66; and religion, 96
Society of Christian Philosophers, 74
South Africa, 136–38
South America. See Latin America
Soviet Union, 18, 121, 122, 147, 149; military, 151–76; weapons, 160–75
Southern Baptists, 71, 84
The Spirit of Enterprise, 64
starvation. See famine
"star wars." See Strategic Defense Initiative
Steinfeld, Jesse L., 39
Strategic Arms Limitation Talks agreement (SALT), 157–59
Strategic Defense Initiative (SDI), 166–75

Suez crisis, 154
Szilard, Leo, 153

Taiwan, 30, 106
technology, 80–81
television, 40–41
teleworking, 27–28
Teller, Edward, 174
Tendler, Moses, 79
Texas, 65, 124; education in, 107–108
Thatcher, Margaret, 139, 148
Third World, 18, 128, 139, 142
Tocqueville, Alexis de, 67, 76, 93, 97–98
Toffler, Alvin, 27
Truman, Harry, 122
Tse-tung, Mao. *See* Mao Tse-tung
Tsongas, Paul, 131
Tube Alloys, 153

unemployment, 24, 30–32
Unification Church, 88
United Church of Christ, 70, 83
United Methodist church, 71, 83
United Nations Food and Agriculture Organization (FAO), 17
U.S. Census Bureau, 42, 54, 56

Vatican Council, Second, 82
Venezuela, 136
Vietnam, 62, 159
Voth, Harold, 40

Wall, Sir Patrick, 149
Wang, An, 63
Wang Laboratories, 63

warfare, 151–76. *See also* weapons; missiles; warheads
warheads, 156–67
Warsaw Pact, 151–71
Washington, D.C., 42, 83, 85
water, 20–22
Wattenberg, Ben, 62
weapons, 153–75; advanced systems of, 162–75
Webber, Alan, 132
Weinberg, Rabbi Joseph, 85
Weinberger, Caspar, 160
welfare, 133–34
Wells, H. G., 153
Western Europe, 23, 138, 140, 151
West Germany: religion in, 68; welfare in, 141
Westinghouse Science Talent Search, 63
Whitehead, Alfred North, 117
Will, George, 132
Wolfe, Thomas, 65
women, 37; Catholic, 82; and education, 115; as heads of households, 42; in ministry, 67, 82–86; and religion, 82–86
The Wonder of Being Human: Our Being and Our Mind, 79
work patterns, 22–29
World Bank, 4, 10, 11, 142
World Future Society, 27
World War I, 163
World War II, 5, 131, 139–40, 150, 153, 163

yuppies, 124

Zen, 90, 127